Also by Robert L. Woodson, Sr.

*Red, White, and Black: Rescuing American History
from Revisionists and Race Hustlers*

Lessons From the Least of These: The Woodson Principles

A PATHWAY
TO AMERICAN
RENEWAL

Red, White, and Black
Volume II

A PATHWAY TO AMERICAN RENEWAL

Red, White, and Black
Volume II

ROBERT L. WOODSON, SR., EDITOR

EMANCIPATION
BOOKS

EMPANCIPATION BOOKS
An Imprint of Post Hill Press
ISBN: 979-8-88845-446-6
ISBN (eBook): 979-8-88845-447-3

A Pathway to American Renewal:
Red, White, and Black Volume II
© 2024 by The Woodson Center
All Rights Reserved

Cover Design by Jim Villaflores

This is a work of nonfiction. All people, locations, events, and situations are portrayed to the best of the author's memory.

Post Hill Press
New York • Nashville
posthillpress.com

Published in the United States of America
1 2 3 4 5 6 7 8 9 10

CONTENTS

PART II: THE EVIDENCE

PART III: THE CHALLENGES

INTRODUCTION

BY ROBERT L. WOODSON, SR.,
FOUNDER AND PRESIDENT,
THE WOODSON CENTER

I am not a scholar. I am a practitioner—a radical pragmatist—who has spent the last fifty years of my life walking among, and learning from, some of the most resilient people you can imagine. They are our anonymous national treasures, embodying the quiet virtues, the resilience, and the fortitude our country most needs to help return us all to the stable foundation we seem to be losing by the day.

In the past and in the present, our forgotten fellow citizens have provided a living testimony that suffering and affliction are not the final word. People have and can recover from internal brokenness and horrendous external assaults on their personhood. In these many years as President of the Woodson Center, I have documented what they have done in order to discover what the rest of us might do. I have learned to identify the common elements of their triumph. And I have learned that the proper way to document and record their success involves listening intently to their accounts rather than coming at them with preconceived programs and theories about what has gone wrong, and why. They tell me—in their own words—what has gone right, and why. Their stories form the core of this volume.

This book—a celebration of resilience—is divided into three sections:

The History: the gritty, painful but often triumphant account of what blacks accomplished at the end of slavery—amazing increases in literacy, family formation, and income. As scholar Josh Mitchell points out, Alexis de Tocqueville wrote almost two centuries ago that America's unique strength was in the way its citizens formed voluntary associations—mediating institutions of family, churches, fraternal organizations. This has been demonstrated most vigorously in the black community. Schools, thriving businesses, and civil rights accomplishments were some of the results they achieved, even in times of rampant prejudice and violence against blacks.

The Evidence: Our grassroots leaders have overcome slavery in the most extreme circumstances of poverty. They have hurdled countless barriers to achievement, including their own addiction, predatory behavior, and prison. Many use their own experiences to teach others, themselves becoming mediation institutions. And if they can find redemption in the midst of some of the most toxic neighborhoods in America, they have much to teach even those living in the gilded ghettos who have all of the comforts of life, and yet live with an internal poverty that haunts them. In their own words in this volume, they provide the incontrovertible evidence of Tocqueville's observation that "democracy unleashes an energy never before seen in human civilization." Our goal is to celebrate and renew that energy.

The Challenges: What happened to the progress made up until the middle of the twentieth century? The Great Society programs of the 1960s undermined the mediating institutions that helped blacks survive—and thrive—against the odds. In recent years, there has been an acceptance of a view that says statistical disparities are caused by systemic racism. Thus, a new mindset has crept in: the problem, some believe, can be fixed by lowering standards—in education, even in the judicial system. This has created a soft and pernicious bigotry of lowered expectations. And as our scholars point out, while the civil rights movement fought for rights enshrined in the Bill of Rights, many current protests call for benefits not earned but demanded.

The central question for today cries out for an answer: how can we rebuild our communities, so our citizens and our nation can be renewed? I am convinced that the least among us point the way forward for us all. I invite you to join me in seeking to recover and transmit the ancient wisdom that suffering and hardship can indeed be overcome. The time for arguments has passed; let us find and support the living proof that this is so.

PART I:
THE HISTORY

I

REBUILDING WHAT WAS LOST

BY RACHEL FERGUSON, PH.D.

The mistake of the far left in pushing back on the concept of resilience is they think that we're just asking hurting people to grit their teeth through the pain. Instead, shalom, or wholeness, means that we are walking alongside our neighbors to empower them in their healing and in their economic uplift.

O ne misconception about the American tradition that one often hears is its hyper-individualism. An emphasis on resilience or grit will often get one accused of a failure to understand the importance of community, social structures, or even just history! On the other hand, progressive accounts of history can devolve into mere trauma-porn, instilling in our young people a sense of racially-coded hopelessness for the future of our country and the efficacy of their individual efforts.

But the critics have really got the American tradition wrong. Alexis de Tocqueville said that while Britons will solve a problem by appealing to some great lord, and the French will work through the government, Americans will start a club. Between the coercion of the state and the incentives of the market lies the wide world of civil society: our families, friendships, clubs, philanthropic efforts, and all of those forms of voluntary association that so enrich our lives. We are a country of "little platoons," and no community offers a better historical example of this characteristic than Black Americans. An unbiased review of Black American history conveys both frustration and hope.

Black American "self-help" has always been communal in nature, with individual efforts supported and networked throughout the community to lift each other up. Black Americans developed genuine resilience by having strong families, churches, schools, fraternal associations, and business networking groups. No man is an island, and true grit doesn't come from mere white-knuckling to reach a goal. Instead, young Black Americans thrive when they are part of healthy communities that shape them, mentor them, educate them, and empower them, which is why projects of neighborhood stabilization must be at the heart of our efforts to encourage resilience.

The Black Church

Lincoln and Mamiya, in *The Black Church in the African American Experience*,[1] call the historical Black church the "cultural womb" of Black America. While still enslaved, many joyfully converted during the famous tent meetings of the Great Awakenings, taking the good news back to their fellows. For the enslaved, the gospel wasn't just the good news that their sins were forgiven through the death and resurrection of Jesus. It also affirmed that they were made in the image of God, with equal worth and dignity to anyone else on earth; that God cares about freedom (both physical and spiritual) and demonstrated such when He liberated the Hebrews from Egyptian oppression and that Jesus himself was a man of sorrows who enters into our suffering.

---

[1]   C. Eric Lincoln and Lawrence H. Mamiya, *The Black Church in the African American Experience* (Durham: Duke University Press, 1990).

Meeting in secret at night, the gospel awakened them to their own self-esteem and to a dream of freedom. But more specifically, it awakened them to a deep and abiding desire to learn how to read the Bible.

After Emancipation, freedmen dashed to do two things as quickly as they could: officially marry their spouses and join a church. These churches, together with philanthropic help from the North, started hundreds of schools. By 1930, a population that was almost completely illiterate in 1865 had reached 80 percent literacy! Economic historian Robert Higgs asserts that this may have been the most rapid leap forward in literacy of any group in history thus far. The church became the hub of community activity, grounding Black uplift in a beautiful heritage of faith.

Business Networks

In the face of immense obstacles post-Reconstruction, great leaders like Booker T. Washington determined that freedmen should become economically independent through a massive educational effort. Washington was strategic; he knew that if they moved North their jobs would unionize and "the black man would be pushed to the wall." So he determined to stay in the South despite its challenges, which meant that he had to use extreme caution as he built up Tuskegee Institute in Alabama. As he had been taught at Hampton Institute in Virginia, where he was trained, property ownership would be the key to forward movement for the community. Through his National Negro Business League, entrepreneurs created funding and advertising networks, and began building real economic capital in the community.

In *Black Liberation Through the Marketplace*,[2] my co-author Marcus Witcher and I dub Washington the "father of the long civil rights movement." After all, without lawyers and businesspeople to fund and staff it, there would have been no NAACP—the National Association for the Advancement of Colored People. It was the great haircare millionaire, Madame C. J. Walker, that gave the NAACP its earliest large financial gift. It was the great publishing magnate, John H. Johnson, who made the fateful decision to publish the pictures of Emmett Till's body in *Jet Magazine*. The hospital entrepreneur, T. R. M. Howard, launched some of the first strategic meetings of the civil rights movement and mentored Fannie Lou Hamer and Medgar Evers. He also played a central role in the Till case by providing his huge, high-security estate for investigation work and the protection of Mamie Till during the trial. Incredibly wise and prescient, Washington knew that economic clout meant the genuine ability to stand up for one's political rights as well.

Fraternal Organizations

From the 1880s to the mid-twentieth century, Black Americans all over the nation created fraternal organizations such as the Black Elks. Another oft-forgotten element of the long civil rights movement, these secret societies allowed for all sorts of organizations, from business to politics, as well as mutual aid. In fact, they served as a kind of early insurance, in which any member received as a benefit the coverage of his family's funeral expenses should he pass away, or monetary help should he be temporarily too ill to work. The future lawyers of the NAACP trained under the fraternal orders, which sued for the right to use the names of already established white orders. Because

---

[2] Rachel S. Ferguson and Marcus M. Witcher, *Black Liberation Through the Marketplace: Hope, Heartbreak, and the Promise of America* (Emancipation Books, 2022).

banding together in their orders made it possible for these Black men to assert some kind of public presence, they became the greatest source of funding for the NAACP, and the natural recruits for the tenfold increase in NAACP membership during World War II. In the 1920s, these organizations had over two million members and $20 million in property, which included headquarters, banks, hospitals, and social welfare institutions.

What Went Wrong?

Many of us will be familiar with the truly stunning statistics on Black employment and the Black family from the 1950s, which show that Black Americans were just as stable as other American citizens. From 1948 to 1966, in fact, Black poverty was cut in half, from almost 90 percent of Black Americans living below the poverty line to fewer than half. Considering that civil rights legislation was only being passed at the tail end of this period, what could possibly explain this economic achievement? I would contend that the Herculean efforts of Black Americans over the previous hundred years to rebuild their families, to center their lives in the church, to educate themselves, and to work toward economic independence allowed them to ride the wave of the 1950s economic boom into the beginnings of the American dream.

But then something went terribly wrong. Families were undermined by the contraception shock and the new morality of the Sexual Revolution. Unions, which had only recently even allowed Blacks to be members, drove jobs off-shore or into automation sooner than they might have, removing from many Black American men that transitional manufacturing job from the manual labor-to-white collar labor journey for many Black American men. And men were again undermined as the rise of the welfare state severely disincentivized marriage.

The massive federal projects of Urban Renewal and the Federal Highway System mowed through poor but upwardly mobile Black economic centers in city after city. In a shockingly short period of time, the burgeoning greatness of the Black American community was hit with this maelstrom of challenges, and many gains were lost.

This narrative should not be overstated. Today, the majority of Black Americans are middle class. Black Americans wield many times the economic power of even the richest of African nations. But too often that power is spent on consumption rather than on building wealth. Too often the wealth building capacity of Black Americans is undermined by destabilized family structures. Our most struggling communities are cut off economically and culturally from those around them. We have this incredibly rich history of healthy community to draw upon, but how can we reinvigorate it today?

Neighborhood Stabilization

Substantive civil society institutions can often be hard to describe, because so much of what happens within them is organic. People meet one another and begin to problem-solve, create, and build, because they have created a milieu in which this is the expected focus. In contrast, isolated or ghettoized communities or unrooted, transient individuals can rarely achieve transformational change. In the last several decades a whole literature around neighborhood stabilization has sprung up to capture the kind of holistic efforts that can bring real healing. Many of these practitioners use the term "shalom" to describe their goal—not merely peace, but wholeness. So many of our government and private efforts seem almost nefariously designed to string recipients along into a lifetime of dependence. We need a paradigm shift!

The first thing that must shift is our attitude. Do we see our needy neighbors as mere recipients, helpless to chart a path for themselves?

Or do we see them as interesting, creative individuals whose dreams have merely been silenced? As my friend Ismael Hernandez puts it, "I'm not interested in your poverty. I'm interested in you." This matter of attitude will affect all of our efforts. If we take the first view, we will not listen to our neighbors, we will not ask them about their vision, we will take up a giveaway, hand-out attitude to any help we bring. If we take the second view, we will always look for opportunities for exchange. We will want to discover people's talents and gifts so that they can pursue their particular vocation. To quote Robert Lupton, author of *Toxic Charity*,[3] "We will subordinate our own agenda to the agenda of our neighbors. Too often, both the state and private philanthropists assume that they know what people really need when they're not even very familiar with the community. Then they get frustrated when their ham-fisted efforts inevitably fail."

The second thing we must shift is our sense of scale. There are no push-button answers to decades and decades of misguided policy that will suddenly turn around the devastating situation in so many of our most destabilized communities. Instead, we will accomplish much by going small and deep as opposed to big and shallow. Focusing on a particular block and dedicating a decade to its stabilization allows us to gain the trust of neighbors, understand issues of territorialism, police relations, and other sensitive facts that should dictate our strategy. While this may seem frustratingly slow, recall that in fifty years of massive and broad one-size-fits-all efforts we have not merely failed but have made the situation far worse. How much better if donors, churches, and non-profits were to turn their attention to this hyper-local model that we know really works. How many neighborhoods could be transformed?

The third thing we need is deep, personal presence. There simply is no way to restore the resilience of our neighbors by staying far

---

[3]   Robert D. Lupton, *Toxic Charity: How the Church Hurts Those They Help and How to Reverse It* (San Francisco: HarperOne, 2011).

away, but sending them checks or clothes. People need people. Our neighbors need someone they can call at midnight when another child has lost his or her life. They need someone who can stick with them when the rage and frustration of so many wounds finally break open. They need someone who knows them well enough to say, "I see how gifted you are in this area. How can I help you develop that?"

I don't mean to imply that every sincere helper needs to move to the inner city! Instead, find those that do and be their network to the wider world outside of that isolated block. Kids, dads, moms, employees, entrepreneurs—they all need mentors and the kinds of connection to opportunities and knowledge that most of us simply take for granted. We can provide that mentorship and connection.

The mistake of the far left in pushing back on the concept of resilience is they think that we're just asking hurting people to grit their teeth through the pain. Instead, shalom, or wholeness, means that we are walking alongside our neighbors to empower them in their healing and in their economic uplift. We collaborate as fellow members of the community, not as know-it-alls or rescuers. What we find when we do this are neighbors with deep reservoirs of strength and spiritual wisdom. We find astounding gifts and talents simply hidden or undeveloped till now. In a cultural moment defined by loneliness, we too find blessing and community. That's because people are not mere recipients—they are unique unrepeatable beings with an eternal destiny. When we dignify our neighbors, they themselves become the givers.

2

ALABAMA'S VOTING RIGHTS STRUGGLE, THE FIRST RECONSTRUCTION: DREAMS DEFERRED

BY JANICE ROGERS BROWN, J.D., LL.M,
RETIRED CIRCUIT JUDGE

*Fraud, violence and discriminatory procedures denied
the ballot to black citizens in southern states, but
these stratagems could not have succeeded absent the
Supreme Court's willingness to nullify Congressional
efforts to punish violence, prevent fraud, and prohibit the constitutional abridgement of the franchise.*

I t was always a longshot. Free people. Self-government. A notion of human equality based on the fatherhood of God and the brotherhood of man. It was a novel idea, risky, and tainted even at its inception by compromise. In an 1820 letter to a Maine politician, Thomas Jefferson analogized America's pact with slavery to having "a wolf by the ears" and being unable to "hold him, nor safely let him go."[4] Jefferson feared slavery would destroy the union and the cataclysm he feared, the Civil War, did exact a bloody retribution.

President Abraham Lincoln at first insisted the war was an effort to restore the national union and nothing more. And despite a vigorous dissent from Northern abolitionists, most white people, including Union soldiers, agreed with him. Congress added its imprimatur by adopting the Crittenden Resolution asserting that the North fought "only to preserve the Union and posed no threat to Southern institutions."[5]

Eventually, however, the necessities of war completely undermined the Union's commitment to leave the South's peculiar institution unscathed. Congress passed two Confiscation Acts, the first allowing the army to use black men and women as military laborers, and the second authorizing the President to employ persons of African descent in any capacity to suppress the rebellion. The Militia Act allowed black men to be employed in any military or naval service and granted freedom to such men and their families.

In the north, Frederick Douglass was one of several well-known public figures who personally recruited free black men, helping to enlist some—including his own son—in the newly formed Fifty-Fourth Massachusetts Regiment.[6] He exhorted black men to help strike the decisive blow, breaking the chains themselves. Douglass believed that once these men fought to preserve the Union, "no power on earth [could] deny that they had earned the right to citizenship in the United States."[7] An editorial in the *Christian Record*, in June 1863, echoed what many volunteers believed. The way to the ballot

---

4   Thomas Jefferson, "Letter to John Holmes," April 22, 1820, Teaching American History, https://teachingamericanhistory.org/document/letter-to-john-holmes-2/.

5   Ira Berlin, Barbara J. Fields, Steven Miller, Joseph Reidy, and Leslie Rowland, *Slaves No More: Three Essays on Emancipation and the Civil War,* (New York: Cambridge University Press, 1992), 17.

6   Leon E. Litwack, *Been in the Storm So Long,* (New York: Random House, 1979), 73.

7   Ibid. 72.

box, into the classroom, and onto the streetcar was "through the battlegrounds of the Confederacy."

Black men—both slave and free—filled the ranks of the Union army. After passage of the Confiscation Acts and issuance of Lincoln's Emancipation Proclamation in January of 1863, black regiments proliferated. "Enlistment not only strengthened the bondman's claim to freedom; it also enhanced the freeman's claim to equality."[8,9]

Despite being subjected to the inequities and indignities which plagued life for all people of African ancestry,[10] black soldiers remained steadfast and loyal to the Union cause, showing courage and initiative, acquitting themselves so well a growing number of white Northerners became convinced that the service and sacrifice of black soldiers entitled them to participate in governing the reconstructed Confederate states.[11] Indeed, in 1864, President Lincoln, writing to the first free-state governor of Louisiana, suggested the franchise might be extended to some of the colored people—"for instance, the very intelligent, and especially those who have fought gallantly in our ranks."[12] He thought "[t]hey would probably help, in some trying time to come, to keep the jewel of liberty within the family of freedom."

Many thought the surrender of the Confederate army at Appomattox signaled a clear and decisive victory for the Union. Both General Ulysses S. Grant and Lt. Col. Joshua Chamberlain, the man directed to choreograph the actual surrender, were determined to treat the rebels with dignity. "General Grant wanted a simple ceremony, one that would not 'humiliate the manhood' of the vanquished army."[13] Secession and rebellion went down, Chamberlain

---

8 Berlin et al, *Slaves No More*, 207.
9 Ibid. 215.
10 Ibid. 189.
11 Ibid. 231-232.
12 Fawn Brodie, *Thaddeus Stevens: Scourge of the South*, (New York: W. W. Norton & Company, 1966), 194.
13 Alice Rains Trulock, *In the Hands of Providence*, (Chapel Hill: The University of North Carolina Press, 1992), 302.

later explained, and slavery, too, was vanquished, because "slavery and freedom cannot live together." He admitted the North "did not go into that fight to strike slavery directly…but God, in His providence, in His justice…set slavery in the forefront, and it was swept aside as with a whirlwind."[14] Chamberlain fervently believed the defeated "were men of honor and their word of honor could be trusted."[15] No one wanted to see an interminable Civil War of skirmishes and guerilla tactics. However, the celebration for escaping that fate was premature. Lee's army surrendered, but the people of the South never accepted defeat.

As Professor James Hogue explains:

> After Lee's surrender at Appomattox, Confederate soldiers never again took up arms in the hope of winning Southern independence from the United States. Nonetheless, their willingness to take up arms after 1865 became the cornerstone for numerous campaigns against local and state governments in the South which helped overthrow Reconstruction's achievements 'from the bottom up.' While not every Confederate veteran became a violent enemy of reconstruction, every violent campaign against Reconstruction crystallized around the leadership and participation of Confederate veterans.[16]

For the south, Civil War historian George Rable observes, "peace became war carried on by other means."[17]

---

[14] Ibid.

[15] Ibid. 303.

[16] James K. Hogue, "The 1873 Battle of Colfax: Paramilitarism and Counterrevolution in Louisiana," 6/27/2006, 6.

[17] George C. Rable, *But There Was No Peace: The Role of Violence in the Politics of Reconstruction* (University of Georgia Press 1984), 15.

The result was a century-long proxy war waged—at first slyly and then confidently—against an impoverished and often rootless caste. The war was not completely one-sided. There were black Union veterans who were armed, organized, politically aware, and who fought back against armed vigilante, paramilitary, and Conservative militia attacks.[18] They were invariably outgunned and outmanned. More ominously, white men could murder black people without any fear of criminal consequences. If a black man injured or killed his assailant, no claim of self-defense would be entertained.

Congressman Thaddeus Stevens, perhaps the most committed among the Radical Republicans to equality under law for the freedmen, regarded the Fourteenth Amendment as a weak, watered-down compromise. The Amendment's central aim was to ensure "equality before the law, overseen by the national government." for black Americans.[19]

The Reconstruction Congress enacted three broad constitutional amendments designed to eliminate the legal disabilities that hobbled the newly freed black male population. The Thirteenth Amendment finished the work of the Emancipation Proclamation and abolished slavery in 1865. Clearly understanding that freedom was not enough, Congress enacted the Fourteenth Amendment, which conferred birthright citizenship on slaves and their descendants and mandated equal protection of the laws and due process. This notion of equality before the law had not previously existed, and Congress included specific mechanisms to ensure its implementation, including Section 5, which authorized Congress to implement the amendment by appropriate legislation. The Fifteenth Amendment prohibited racial discrimination in voting rights.

---

[18] Hogue, *Battle of Colfax*, 5-6.
[19] Ernest A. Young, "Dying Constitutionalism and the Fourteenth Amendment," *Marquette Law Review, Vol. 102, Issue 3, Spring 2019*, 952.

Arguably, the centerpiece of the Radical Republicans' strategy was access to the ballot.[20] Congressman Stevens had reluctantly agreed with Frederick Douglass's impassioned argument that "the school house door would never open for the Negro unless he had the ballot."[21] Although the Fifteenth Amendment was not self-executing, its anti-discrimination provision—together with the Equal Protection clause of the Fourteenth—arguably outlawed literacy, property, character requirements, and other similar obstacles to voting.

Moreover, the Military Reconstruction Act of 1867 granted the franchise to black residents in ten Southern states. Within two months of the Fifteenth Amendment's passage, Republicans in Congress sought to protect every male citizen's right to vote against interference through violence, intimidation, or bribery by any persons or groups, official or unofficial.[22] As historian C. Vann Woodward summed up the Radicals' efforts: "[so] far as humanly possible to do by statute and constitutional amendment, America would seem to have been firmly committed to the principle of equality."[23] And yet, as he acknowledges, "within a very short time after these imposing commitments were made they were broken. America reneged, shrugged off the obligation, and all but forgot about it for nearly a century."[24]

Congress' efforts were not entirely ineffective. Black voters [did elect] "state legislators and congressmen—about a sixth of the total—from the eleven states that actually joined the Confederacy" and they composed perhaps "a quarter of the delegates to the ten state conventions that reshaped the southern constitutional order between 1867 and 1869."[25]

---

20 Morgan Kousser, *The Voting Rights Act and the Two Reconstructions* (Athens: University of Georgia Press, 1991), 4.

21 Brodie. *Thaddeus Stevens*, 211-212.

22 Ibid. 7.

23 C. Vann Woodward, "Equality: The Deferred Commitment," in *The Burden of Southern History*, 2nd ed. (Baton Rouge: LSU Press, 1993), 69, 75.

24 Ibid. 78-79.

25 Morgan, *The Voting Rights Act*, 9.

While publicly agreeing to the new amendments, most public officials in the former Confederate states made only token efforts to comply and vigorously resisted Reconstruction with violence, fraud, and deceit. Vigilante action was directed at schools, churches, and Republican officials, as well as freedmen and their families.[26] Even before the passage of the Civil War Amendments, Freedmen's Bureau officials and the generals in charge of military districts reported many murders and lynchings, as well as rapes and other mayhem.

Though Abraham Lincoln truly harbored "malice toward none" and was inclined to offer a general amnesty to the secessionists, he felt universal amnesty "must rest on the principle of civil and political equality of both races."[27] Lincoln's assassination ended the discussion of amnesty. Andrew Johnson, an unrepentant racist, made so many efforts to derail Reconstruction that he barely survived impeachment.

Fortunately, when General Ulysses S. Grant became president, he pledged to do all he could to "advance the best interests" of American citizens "without regard to color." President Grant committed federal resources to ensuring black welfare, generously funding the Bureau of Education created to educate freed people.[28] When the Fifteenth Amendment became law, Grant sent a special message to Congress, calling its ratification "the most important event since the nation came into life."[29] Later, he said, "It looked to me as the realization of the Declaration of Independence."[30] But, the ink was hardly dry on the amendment before southern demagogues began plotting ways to circumvent it.

The Klan "launched a new civil war by clandestine means."[31] In terrifying midnight raids, black people were dragged from their

---

[26] Hogue, *Battle of Colfax*, 6.
[27] Brodie, *Thaddeus Stevens*, 227, citing a letter from Lincoln to General Wadsworth.
[28] Ron Chernow, *Grant* (New York: Penguin Books, 2017), 657.
[29] Ibid. 685.
[30] Ibid. 686.
[31] Ibid. 702.

homes and whipped; entire families of Republicans were murdered. Alabama's reconstruction governor William Smith complained, "things look here very much as they did in 1860."[32]

Violence did provoke countermeasures such as the recruitment of Radical state militias (including black militias) and the intervention of the U.S. Army. The newly created Department of Justice,[33] headed by a fearless and determined Attorney General, Amos Ackerman, faced the daunting task of enforcing the Civil War Amendments and suppressing the White Citizens Council—the Ku Klux Klan.

Grant was inundated with letters describing the harrowing violence overtaking southern towns. Grant responded by personally beseeching Congress to pass legislation to stop this domestic terrorism. Despite strong opposition from Democrats, Grant's vigorous lobbying was rewarded by passage of the Third Enforcement Act, giving him extraordinary powers to suspend *habeas corpus*, declare martial law and send in troops.

True to his promises, Grant smashed the initial incarnation of the Klan so thoroughly that Frederick Douglass rejoiced that the "scourging and slaughter of our people have so far ceased."[34] But, it was not enough to fulfill the promise of Reconstruction. As Ackerman balefully acknowledged: "I doubt whether from the beginning of the world until now, a community, nominally civilized, has been so fully under the domination of systematic and organized depravity."[35]

Fraud, violence and discriminatory procedures denied the ballot to black citizens in Southern states, but these stratagems could not have succeeded absent the Supreme Court's willingness to nullify Congressional efforts to punish violence, prevent fraud, and prohibit the constitutional abridgement of the franchise.

---

[32]   Ibid.702-703.
[33]   Hogue, *Battle of Colfax*, 6-7.
[34]   Ibid. at 709.
[35]   Ibid.

Beginning with the *Slaughterhouse* case in 1873 and continuing well into the twentieth century, the Court proceeded to nullify most of the benefits the Civil War amendments had intended to confer on the freedmen and, with the end of Reconstruction, did more than any other federal institution to snatch defeat from the jaws of victory. Although the South had lost the Civil War, the court made sure "it conquered the constitutional law."[36]

The Supreme Court significantly affected the constitutional landscape by striking down the 1875 Civil Rights Act's prohibition of discrimination in public accommodations in the *Civil Rights Cases*,[37] and upholding state segregation laws in *Plessy v. Ferguson*.[38] But, the court's own counterrevolution started much earlier.

In two opinions in 1876, the Court undermined Congress' attempt to protect all citizens against violence and fraud, state sponsored or private, in connection with local elections. In *U.S. v. Reese*,[39] Kentucky officials refused to accept the ballots of citizens because they were black. *Reese* was the first test of the 1870-1872 Enforcement Acts that were devised to effectuate the protections of the Civil War Amendments. Election inspectors, Reese and Foushee, refused to allow William Garner, an African American, to vote in Lexington's municipal election because he had failed to pay a $1.50 tax. Garner had attempted to pay the tax, but the tax collector refused it. Under the 1870 Enforcement Act, if an official refused to permit a citizen to complete an action required for voting, the citizen could present an affidavit. Reese and Foushee refused to accept Garner's affidavit. They were indicted, but the circuit court found the relevant section of the Enforcement Act exceeded the bounds of the Fifteenth Amendment and dismissed the indictments.

---

[36] Robert J. Harris, *The Quest for Equality* (Baton Rouge: Louisiana State University Press, 1960), 108.
[37] 109 U.S. 3 (1883).
[38] 163 U.S. 537 (1896).
[39] 92 U. S. 214 (1876).

In an eight-to-one decision authored by Chief Justice Waite, the Supreme Court agreed. The court said the language was not sufficiently tailored to qualify as "appropriate legislation." As Justice Hunt pointed out in dissent, this was a ludicrous misapplication of an elementary canon of statutory construction. "Statutes must be so construed as to make all parts harmonize and give sensible effect to each." An examination of surrounding circumstances, knowledge of the evil to be prevented, and a clear statement of the acts prohibited and made punishable, stated a sufficient offense against the United States and constituted appropriate legislation under the Fifteenth Amendment. The Court's strained interpretation in *Reese* enabled states to deny the vote to blacks based on poll taxes, literacy, character and other tests.

In *U.S. v. Cruikshank*,[40] Louisiana indicted and convicted some of the perpetrators of the Colfax riot—the largest racial mass murder in American history.[41] William B. Cruikshank was one of the men convicted. On appeal to the Supreme Court, the convictions were reversed. In another majority decision written by Waite, the court held that Congress had power, under the Fourteenth Amendment, to prohibit states from denying life, liberty or property without due process of law but was powerless to protect freemen when they were assaulted or murdered by private citizens. The Cruikshank decision gave a green light to terrorism wherever local officials could not or would not enforce the law. Indeed, James Beckwith, the U.S. Attorney who had drawn up the initial indictment, wrote to inform the U.S. Attorney General that various White League organizations "had sprung to life and grown influential" precisely because of the decision.

In *Williams v. Mississippi*,[42] the Supreme Court unanimously upheld provisions in Mississippi's 1890 Constitution providing

---

[40]   92 U.S. 542 (1876).
[41]   Kousser, *Voting Rights Act*, 23.
[42]   170 U.S. 213 (1898).

for a poll tax, literacy tests, and a grandfather clause, because they were not facially discriminatory. Although Williams's lawyer quoted extensively from the 1890 disfranchising convention to demonstrate the state's racist intent, the court said as long as the provisions were facially neutral and could be applied to all individuals regardless of race, the Fourteenth Amendment was satisfied. To prevail, William would have to show proof of actual discrimination.

As much damage as the *Reese, Cruikshank, Williams* trilogy did to voting rights, the Court was still not done. A case which established both discriminatory intent and effect arose in Shelby County, Alabama. In *Giles v. Harris*,[43] Jackson Giles, head of the Colored Men's Suffrage Association, challenged the enfranchisement provisions of the 1901 Alabama Constitution. Giles argued the Constitution had been "proposed and ratified by a racist and biased group of elite Democrats intent on disfranchising African Americans." As Samuel Brenner notes, these types of constitutional conventions proliferated after the end of Reconstruction, and Southern politicians were not shy about describing their intentions. Although Senator "Pitchfork Ben" Tillman acknowledged that in four bloody years of civil war—when slaves were in charge of the wives, children, and homes of confederate soldiers—"not one solitary crime was reported against them," he took pride in convening a constitutional convention for the sole purpose of disenfranchising as many [black people] as we could under the Fourteenth and Fifteenth Amendments."[44] For Senator Tillman, and his ilk, reversing the gains of Reconstruction constituted redemption.

The new Alabama Constitution served the same purpose. Voters, all of whom had to pay a poll tax, were divided into two groups. One group, mostly all white, who were qualified to register prior to

---

[43]   189 U. S. 475 (1903).
[44]   Benjamin R. Tillman, Speech in the Senate on "The Disenfranchisement of African Americans," March 23, 1900, *Congressional Record, 56th Congress, 1st Session,* 3223-3224.

December 20, 1902, only had to register once, through an easy process, to be qualified to vote for life. The voters in the second group, mostly nonwhite, had to face a system of harsh and discretionarily applied literacy, employment, and property tests, administered for each election. Voters in the second group had to overcome greater hurdles than the first group and had to do it over and over again. The system worked exactly as intended. "[O]f the 181,471 eligible African American voters in 1900, only 3000 were registered under the new constitutional provisions."[45]

Notwithstanding the stark nature of the facts, the Supreme Court denied relief. Justice Oliver Wendall Holmes said the court could do nothing, because suffrage is a political question. Thus, the court eviscerated the racial equality purpose of the Reconstruction Amendments and set the stage for "legally-mandated, state-based apartheid...."[46]

Mr. Jefferson's intuition was accurate. Still, neither he nor other members of the founding generation could have imagined that years of war, rivers of blood, and the sacrifice of some of the best and brightest of a generation would not be enough. The depravity Amos Ackerman lamented in the war-ravaged generation of Southerners became a cherished legacy of entitlement passed on to their descendants.[47] The grandchildren of black folks—slave and free—who survived the Civil War got an inheritance too. The savage misery of slavery was the leitmotif of their grandparents' sorrow songs and their certitude: black skin did not make people barbaric, cruel, evil, or less than human—black hearts did.

45 Samuel Brenner, "Airbrushed Out of the Constitutional Canon: The Evolving Understanding of Giles v. Harris, 1903-1925," *Vol. 107 Michigan Law Review, Issue 5, 2009,* 853, 859.
46 James W. Fox, "Black Progressivism and the Progressive Court," *Vol. 130, Yale Law Journal, Jan. 2021,* 1.
47 Lillian Smith, *Killers of the Dream* (New York: W.W. Norton & Co. 1994), 89-91, 95-97, 161-163, 164-165.

3

NO WEAPON FORMED AGAINST YOU: RESILIENCE AND THE BLACK CHURCH

BY BISHOP DEAN NELSON

The Black Church is resilient because its purpose transcends time, space, the vapid outrage of the day. It produces resilience in its members because it nourishes us with the eternal and unchanging Word of God, as well as the accumulated wisdom of people who have applied that Word by trusting God in the midst of actual suffering.

One of my earliest church memories is from an Easter sometime in the early 1970s. Barely school-aged and decked out in my new suit and hat, I told my mother as we arrived for service that I needed to use the bathroom. At the time, the bathroom at Salem Baptist Church was an outhouse, which felt less sturdy and thus scarier than the one at my grandparents' home. Mom sent me on my way, and after I finished my business, I couldn't resist the urge to peer down into that dark, smelly, mysterious hole.

Tragically, my brand-new hat slipped off my head and was lost forever to the stench, a casualty of my boyish curiosity. Some five decades later, our family attended Easter at that same building. My adult children chuckled politely as I rehearsed the Easter hat story for them for at least the twentieth time and pointed out where the outhouse used to be.

My parents brought our family to church at least once a week for as long as I can remember. Like all members of the rural congregation, we dressed in our "Sunday Best." For some, this might have involved some profiling, but for all it was a demonstration of our respect for God, for His Church, and for one another. Looking back, it seems obvious that the self-control it took to sit in the pews—under the watchful eye of my parents, the pastor, and the Almighty Himself— was the same self-control it took to sit still in school or right now at the desk where I type these words.

Today, my family's faith remains more than a creed or set of doctrines. It is also a set of practices, of habits, of things we actually do. Salem—its property, history, and people—connects me to a real past, even as my children connect me to a real future I won't see. Salem's sanctuary—built by the offerings and labor of former slaves—might not have the lighting or sound system of our current church, but regular visits there are a good reminder that the faith that sustains us now sustained our forbearers in much more modest circumstances.

The Black Church in America is both a resilient institution as well as an institution that has produced resilient individuals, resilient families and resilient communities. It's not hard to imagine why black Americans would identify with the many stories in the Bible of God being on the side of the oppressed and persecuted. Promises He made to His people that "No weapon formed against you shall prosper, And every tongue *which* rises against you in judgment You shall condemn. This *is* the heritage of the servants of the Lord, And their righteousness *is* from Me"[48] must have offered courage and comfort in the face of slave catchers and water cannons alike.

Of course, not every entity that stands the test of time makes the people it shapes stronger and better; plenty of enduring schools continue to produce barely literate graduates, for example. But for centuries now, the Black Church has proven a powerful refuge against afflictions both historic and modern. Not only did it carry us through slavery and segregation, but it also offers us shelter today from the alienation and hopelessness that afflict so many despite their material prosperity.

Perhaps this is at least in part because the Black American Church was born in adversity. In its earliest days, many whites "…had seriously objected to the evangelization of the Negroes, feeling that they could not be saved and, when the latter had become convinced of this error, many of them were far from the position of conceding to the blacks equality in their church organizations."[49]

Slaveowners began warming to the idea that blacks could receive the salvation Christ offered when some colonies passed laws clarifying that baptizing slaves did not require that they be freed.[50] But to maintain the system of American slavery itself, slaveowners had to prevent their human chattel from forming families or communities. So Christian slaves were typically banned from gathering on their own to practice their faith and instead assembled covertly. In her essay *Black Church History and Urban Apologetics*, Dr. Tiffany Gill explains, "After attending plantation services sanctioned by masters, enslaved believers would often steal away into the woods to participate in

---

[48]   Isaiah 54:17 NKJV Thomas Nelson (2005).

[49]   Carter G. Woodson, *A History of the African American Church* (Diasporic Africa Press, 2017), 37.

[50]   Besheer Mohamed, et al, "A Brief Overview of Black Religious History in the US," Pew Research Center, February 16, 2021, https://www.pewresearch.org/religion/2021/02/16/a-brief-overview-of-black-religious-history-in-the-u-s/.3,Eric Mason, *Urban Apologetics: Restoring Black Dignity with the Gospel* (Zondervan, 2021), 40-41.

secret gatherings, despite slave codes that deemed gatherings of large numbers of Black people illegal."[51]

Salem, like so many black congregations, grew out of such slave prayer meetings. In our case, they began with just two young ladies: Mary E. Ross and Fannie Boyd. According to our church's records, they "continued in their small way, by holding such meetings and receiving great spiritual blessings, in sending up their prayers, wishes and desires to the Almighty God." Miss Ross and Miss Boyd continued to meet after slavery ended, and formally established the church in 1872. They hired a pastor to teach them the Word of God, and the growing congregation raised $4,000 to erect the very building my family and I still visit today.

Only about one hundred years separate the official establishment of Salem and the loss of my hat that Easter; its current pastor is only the eighth to serve in that role. Despite the desire of some to relegate American slavery to the unknowable past, Miss Ross's and Miss Boyd's bondage is about the same distance from my birth as World War I is from today. Deacons and deaconesses who serve today survived Jim Crow. The question—in my mind anyway—isn't whether we should endlessly ponder these past injustices or forget them and move on. It's what lessons we should draw from their proximity.

The lessons I learned from Salem's pulpit were neither a denial of the existence of suffering and injustice nor despair at their presence. I learned, in the words of one of the hymns we sang regularly:

> I'm pressing on the upward way. New heights I'm
> gaining every day.
> Still praying as I onward bound, Lord, plant my feet
> on higher ground.

---

51   Tiffany Gill, "Black Church History and Urban Apologetics," in *Urban Apologetics: Restoring Black Dignity with the Gospel* (Zondervan, 2021).

The meaning of these words is obvious enough. What I want to emphasize is that I sang them—and other hymns with similar messages—from the days of my earliest memories into adulthood, over and over, together with my family and my community. They did more than educate my mind and inform my decision making. They penetrated my soul and, like Miss Ross and Miss Boyd before me, taught me to direct all my prayers, wishes, and desires to the Almighty God.

The seemingly simple directive to "cast all your cares upon Him because He cares for you"[52] actually was a resilient and adaptable life raft that carried much of black America across the stormy sea from enslavement to liberation. The journey was marked by almost infinite variations of the same dilemma: how much oppression do we accept as beyond our control and how much do we fight for change? "Agitate, agitate, agitate," Frederick Douglass urged us, but who can live in a constant state of agitation? And how do we agitate without losing sight of for whom and what we are agitating?

My own grandparents, as well as other members of my church community, seemed to have handled these existential questions with ease. They worked unbelievably hard. With a grade school education, they grew vegetables, kept chickens, and built a business emptying septic tanks. They used all the money they saved to buy land and set up their children and grandchildren for greater economic mobility, all while building a dense kin network that loved and supported itself.

And they were some of the most joyful people I've ever known. They lived in the same world described in James Baldwin's *Letter to My Nephew* or Ralph Ellison's *Invisible Man*, and they navigated its same dangers and frustrations. According to family lore, my grandfather had to bring an armed posse of brothers and cousins to his real estate closings because a lot of people didn't want blacks buying land in Virginia in those days. Yet today, I regularly encounter people of

---

52   1 Peter 5:7 (para). NKJV. Thomas Nelson (2005).

all ages, races, and socioeconomic statuses who do not have a fraction of the peace and contentment they exuded daily. They were simply trusting the Lord to plant their feet on higher ground.

My children face adulthood with a cornucopia of choices that would have been unimaginable to my grandparents. Their challenge is to voluntarily give up some of those options in order to safeguard that elusive joy and to teach their children to do the same. Achievement may occupy the mind, and economic productivity might pay a stranger to care for you in your old age, but neither can love you back. Here again, a lesson from the pulpit and community of my childhood rings in my ears: "I know how to be abased, and I know how to abound. Everywhere and in all things I have learned both to be full and to be hungry, both to abound and to suffer need. I can do all things through Christ who strengthens me."[53]

Although the arson of black churches unfortunately persists, for the most part we face a different kind of opposition today. On the one hand, there are those who would rob us of our cultural distinctiveness, asserting that our country "has moved beyond race," and so unique black American expressions of Christianity are no longer necessary or even desirable. Part of me entertains sympathy for this view; my wife is biracial and our children triracial, so we are hardly primed to see such categories as fundamental to identity or meaning. But ultimately, the Black Church remains uniquely important to millions—including my family and me—because it connects us to our unique past, which, for us at least, holds the key to thriving in the present and future.

Then there are those who would happily allow us to keep our cultural distinctiveness but rob us of our moral peculiarities. The Black Church's pesky devotion to Scriptural inerrancy and affirmation of traditional sexual ethics makes some who would otherwise enjoy our

---

[53]   5 Philippians 4:12, NKJV. Thomas Nelson (2005).

choirs and social activism supremely uncomfortable. If we could just make our faith ornamental instead of foundational, we'd be so much more helpful to their agenda.

In the end, neither of these criticisms matters.

The Black Church is resilient because its purpose transcends time, space, the vapid outrage of the day. It produces resilience in its members because it nourishes us with the eternal and unchanging Word of God, as well as the accumulated wisdom of people who have applied that Word by trusting God in the midst of actual suffering. This wisdom is reflected not just in words from the pulpit, but in the living habits and traditions of the congregations themselves.

Faith and its accompanying values are not transmitted in a vacuum. Book learning certainly plays a role, but for the overwhelming majority of humanity, the habits of the heart and mind must be tethered to the rituals of daily life to take root in any meaningful way. Why would anyone want to discard a repository of millions of testimonies of overcoming life's most challenging obstacles by faith? They are our witnesses, described in Hebrews 12, and they urge us upward and onward, that the Lord would plant our feet on higher ground.

4

HOMOPHILY AND RESILIENCE: HOW BLACK EXCELLENCE IN THE SEGREGATED SOUTH INSPIRED A GENERATION OF JEWISH EUROPEANS

BY JOHN SIBLEY BUTLER, PH.D.

*This strategy of close communities and mutual aid
has been shared by countless immigrant enclaves
over the years…The combination of educational
institutions, business enterprise and savvy to achieve
a better life is the very promise of America and
should be celebrated…it is still open today to all who
would have the courage and tenacity to walk it.*

I am a proud product of the black bourgeoisie, the thriving black middle- and upper-class communities that emerged especially in the segregated South after slavery. We wasted no tears at being shut out from white institutions. Instead, we banded together and built our own, from churches and universities to hotels and resorts. Many people are shocked to learn that I grew up as a black man in Louisiana feeling sorry for the struggling, barely illiterate whites I saw around me. Those same individuals are doubtless unaware that communities like mine served as inspiration for persecuted Jews in early twentieth-century Europe.

Resilience is rarely cultivated in a vacuum. The story of Black American resilience is largely one of homophily, the human tendency to be drawn to those with whom we have something in common. These social ties transcend short term economic interest, meeting the deeper need to belong to a group and confidently rely on its support. In the aftermath of slavery and the midst of Jim Crow, Black Americans like me made progress by sticking together. Several scholars have documented multiple black enclaves' remarkable rise from slavery to success. Leo H. Hirsch, Jr.'s *The Free Negro in New York*, Richard C. Wade's *The Negro in Cincinnati, 1800-1830*, Booker T. Washington's *Durham North Carolina: A City of Negro Enterprises*, and Dennis Kimbro's *The Wealth Choice: Success Secrets of Black Millionaires* are just a few examples of dozens.

Although tragically neglected in too many history books, the meteoric rise of American blacks became an inspiration for oppressed people worldwide. A notable Jewish academic, Max Weinrich, would study these black communities from the segregated South and walk away with a blueprint for how Jewish refugees could survive and thrive amidst the Nazi attempts to subdue and exterminate them in Europe.

Segregation vs Homophily

As my friend and mentor Bob Woodson is fond of saying, the opposite of segregation is desegregation, not forced integration. Countless racial and ethnic groups have found success in America through homophily—building mutually supportive communities with their co-ethnics—rather than rapidly assimilating into the majority culture. From pooling resources to launching small businesses to cram sessions for college entrance exams in church basements, racial and ethnic subcultures have invested in their members—and particularly their children—to advance over generations.

Voluntary homophily is very different from the legalized segregation imposed on black Americans in the wake of the Civil War. In their 2001 work *Birds of a Feather: Homophily in Social Networks*,[54] Miller McPearson, Lynn Smith-Lovin, and James M. Cook demonstrate how various types of homophily create social ties between individuals and structure social networks. Homophily in race and ethnicity creates the strongest networks (and consequently divisions), followed by age, religion, education, occupation and gender. While members of such networks will limit their interactions with outsiders—thus potentially limiting their exposure to future possibilities—understanding the strength they gain from their networks is vital to understanding how those who begin with socioeconomic disadvantages are able to advance in America.

Robust literature on the negative effects of legal segregation abounds. Jim Crow was gravely unjust, robbing newly-freed black population of social, economic and political opportunities. But LeeAnn G. Reynolds' *Maintaining Segregation: Children and Racial Instruction in the South, 1920-1955*, Karl E. Taeuber's *Racial Segregation: The Persisting Dilemma*, and Richard Rothstein's *The Color of Law: A Forgotten History of How Our Government Segregated America* are distinct works, in that they distinguish between segregation and voluntary homophily. They correctly observe that the damaging effect of legal segregation was treating blacks as second-class citizens in the eyes of the law, not depriving them of the presence of whites.

---

[54] Miller McPearson, Lynn Smith-Lovin, and James M. Cook, "Birds of a Feather: Homophily in Social Networks," *Annual Review of Sociology*, Vol. 27:415-444 (2001), https://doi.org/10.1146/annurev.soc.27.1.415.

Nearly all successful groups in America have engaged in homophily to some extent, building distinct mediating structures within their communities. To be sure, different groups experienced different degrees of hostility, and race was just one of many factors that could lead to exclusion from majority dominated institutions. White Latter-Day Saints (LDS) members were excluded from various institutions because of their faith, but they created their own well-known homogenous community in Utah. Ultimately, the discrimination they experienced brought out their best, prompting them to found Brigham Young University and look to the future, as they also built robust businesses that formed the foundation of their current wealth. In her article "Mormons More Faithful with More Education," Katherine Orgill takes note of this model of upward mobility in the face of persecution and prejudice.[55]

Likewise, blacks throughout the US effectively utilized homophily, creating many profoundly successful institutions while being continually denied opportunities in the larger society. For years, both the media and the academy have treated dangerous, low-income black neighborhoods as normative for our community, while paying little to no attention to places like the middle-class black town in southern Louisiana where I grew up. In fact, an examination of data on post-high school education among blacks reveals that in states where legal segregation was the greatest, blacks had the highest percentage of college graduates. Thus, in 1992, as noted in my work *Entrepreneurship and Self-Help Among Black Americans*,[56] 27.9 percent of blacks in Mississippi had college degrees, followed by Louisiana (24.6 percent), Georgia (22.3 percent), South Carolina (21.2 percent), Alabama (20.1 percent), Maryland (18.1 percent), and North Carolina (14.9 percent).

---

[55] Katherine Orgill, "Mormons More Faithful with More Education," *The Daily Universe*, May 5, 2015, https://universe.byu.edu/2015/05/05/final-story-21/.

[56] John Sibley Butler, *Entrepreneurship and Self-Help Among Black Americans: A Reconsideration of Race and Economics* (New York: SUNY Press, 2005).

The Historically Black Colleges and Universities (HBCUs) these students attended predate many predominantly white universities today, undermining the assumption that HBCUs were founded solely to provide an alternative for blacks excluded from white schools. In fact, only a few segments of white Southerners developed the same emphasis on education as black southerners. Nancy Isenberg's *White Trash: the 400 Year History of Class in America*[57] is an outstanding treatment of how most white Americans in the south struggled to build systems of educational and business success in the face of an upper class that considered them inferior.

Of course, homophily is not the only model for upward mobility in America. Many immigrants have also been able to advance in America by rapid assimilation into the majority culture, documented thoroughly in Milton Garden's influential book, *Assimilation in American Life*. Garden details how European immigrants changed their names, religions, and language to mimic the majority and as a result were afforded greater educational and professional opportunities. But black Americans would almost always be physically distinct from whites, even when they successfully adopted mainstream speech patterns and other social customs. In *A Piece of the Pie*, Stanley Lieberson noted that while most European immigrants—after a long process of assimilation—were able to be accepted in mainstream white American society, race prevented most blacks from utilizing this model.[58]

Max Weinreich's Yiddish Scientific Institute

While famous black intellectuals were engaging in philosophical debates about assimilation and segregation in America, oppressed

---

[57] Nancy Isenberg, *White Trash: the 400 Year History of Class in America* (New York: Penguin Books; 2017).

[58] Stanley Lieberson, *A Piece of the Pie: Blacks and White Immigrants Since 1880* (Oakland: University of California Press, 1981).

groups around the world took notice of the success of the black homophily model in the South. This included Jewish Europeans who noted that blacks in the segregated South created a network of private colleges and universities and a group economy, and turned what America called segregation into one of the most dynamic paths to success. History books make much of the Great Migration, devoting many pages to those blacks who left the South. But others discovered principles for resilience and success from those who remained.

The inspiration they took from Booker T. Washington's Tuskegee Machine is recorded in a PBS documentary of Max Weinrich's Yiddish Scientific Institute. Weinreich was a German scholar interested in a path forward for impoverished Jews and their children in the ghettos of Europe. Following World War I, he created the Yiddish Scientific Institute to build resilience, preserve culture, and create economic progress in the face of prejudice. Weinreich understood that upwardly mobile Jews needed to adopt the language of their host country, but with over eight million Jews in countries such as Poland, Latvia, Lithuania, Czechoslovakia, Hungry, and other countries outside of Europe who spoke only Yiddish, he had his work cut out for him.

The best analysis of Weinrich's efforts to meet this challenge is Leila Zenderland's *Weapons of the Weak, Max Weinreich, the Yiddish Scientific Institute, and the Study of Culture, Personality, and Prejudice.*[59] She notes that Weinrich's Yiddish Press closely monitored events from the American South in the early twentieth century; Yiddish writers passionately denounced lynching, riots and racial segregation, while frequently passionately praising African American accomplishments. As Weinreich traveled throughout the South, he knew he had found a model for the Jewish Ghettos in Europe. Zenderland writes:

---

[59] Leila Zenderland, "Social Science as a 'Weapon of the Weak': Max Weinreich, the Yiddish Scientific Institute, and the Study of Culture, Personality, and Prejudice," *Isis* 104, no. 4, (2013), https://www.journals.uchicago.edu/doi/abs/10.1086/674942.

Most inspiring was his visit to Tuskegee Institute in Alabama, a segregated institution founded in the post–Civil War era on an ideology of self-help. While many white academics of the 1930s considered Tuskegee essentially a trade school, Weinreich was enchanted; he would describe this institution in glowing terms at a Yiddish conference in Vilna in 1935. Since its beginnings in a dilapidated shack, Weinreich recounted, Tuskegee had grown to become a proud college that taught technical skills. Most impressive was its extension department, which showed poor farmers better ways to raise poultry, diversify diets, or build outhouses. "When I heard all this," Weinreich exclaimed, "I compared it to the cultural work that we are taking to the provinces," for YIVO lecturers frequently spoke about more abstract subjects such as contemporary literature or art. He himself had "not the slightest doubt as to which method was better," Weinreich added in praising Tuskegee.[60]

Weinreich also visited schools such as Fisk University and was further impressed, interacting with the faculty to discuss and share experiences. He was in awe of how the black network of success turned the intentions of segregation upside down by providing practical paths to success.

Weinreich also shared black leaders' concern that research focusing on a population's deficiencies could easily be weaponized against the Jewish population in Europe, as it had been (and continues to be) against black Americans. As noted by Zenderland, "As social

---

[60] Zenderland, "Social Science as a 'Weapon of the Weak'"

scientists from vulnerable communities soon discovered, such weapons were usually double-edged. Producing knowledge that exposed social or psychological weaknesses could be dangerous, for it could also supply ammunition to one's enemies. This paradox often left the leaders of these communities wary of if not hostile to such research."[61]

Indeed, this same hazard had led W.E.B. Dubois to switch to a data collection that included not only the struggles of a black community, as was the hallmark of *The Philadelphia Negro*,[62] to also writing *The College Bred Negro and Economic Co-Operation Among Negroes*.[63] After returning from his studies in Germany, he noted that many white readers gleefully read about bastards and prostitutes in his *Philadelphia Negro*, which seemed to confirm their very worse assumptions about black Americans. Continuing such an approach, he feared, would create amusement, contempt, and pity among non-black readers and would also be used by the state to justify continued discrimination. Because of this belief, DuBois dropped his deficiency-oriented analysis of the black community and collected data that also documented success. Weinreich took note of this to better understand how Germany utilized social science against Jews in the ghetto. Like DuBois, this revelation changed the trajectory of his research and his 1946 book, *Hitler's Professors*,[64] where he demonstrated how Nazis exploited the language and methods of social science to justify antisemitism. Hitler's Final Solution, to Weinreich, was in some ways a logical extension of presenting only the negative side of data gathered about a people group.

---

[61] Ibid.

[62] W.E.B. Dubois, *The Philadelphia Negro: A Social Study* (Philadelphia: University of Pennsylvania Press, 1995).

[63] E.B. Dubois, *Economic Co-Operation Among Negro Americans* (Forgotten Books, 2018).

[64] Max Weinreich, *Hitler's Professors: The Part of Scholarship in Germany's Crimes Against the Jewish People* (New Haven: Yale University Press, 1946).

Conclusion

Since the inception of America, blacks have developed many models of success. Free blacks from New York to New Orleans provided a way for the future for their communities by developing strong business communities held together by homophily. After slavery, many blacks went north to the cities until the work disappeared. But those who stayed under intense southern segregation, built colleges, universities and other mediating institutions to create a path forward for their children. This strategy of close communities and mutual aid has been shared by countless immigrant enclaves over the years, and it was this model of black success that Max Weinreich took back to Germany. The combination of educational institutions, business enterprise, and savvy to achieve a better life is the very promise of America and should be celebrated. It is the path to success I myself walked, and it is still open today to all who would have the courage and tenacity to walk it.

5

BUILDING BLOCKS
OF RESILIENCY

BY WILL CROSSLEY, M.ED., PH.D.,
THE PINEY WOODS SCHOOL

There will be times in your life when things logically won't make sense, and you will wonder, 'Do I keep going?' The impetus to keep going is the realization that God does not call us to be successful; He calls us to be faithful.

How do we become resilient? Perhaps we have no greater principle for living than resilience. We live complicated and disruptive lives, with our pathways never completely smooth. Sometimes the only principle available to us will be our ability to bounce back from our mistakes, losses, and disappointments. Resilient men and women, such as Laurence Clifton Jones and Grace Allen Jones, who founded The Piney Woods Country Life School, move forward after repeated setbacks because they have a vision—a purpose—and know that pursuing this cause is more important than their momentary distress. Piney Woods, a youth leadership farm community in rural Mississippi, is the nation's longest-serving historically Black boarding program.

This skill—the art of being resilient—must be honed, developed by enduring pressure again and again. Once honed, resilience becomes a frame of mind, an attitude, an approach to life. This honing begins with a choice—specifically, how to respond to unwelcome situations.

Holocaust survivor Viktor Frankl said in his book, *Man's Search for Meaning*, "Everything can be taken from a man but one thing: the last of the human freedoms—to choose one's attitude in any given set of circumstances, to choose one's own way."[65]

Frankl speaks to a chosen internal disposition that allows a person to get back up after being knocked down repeatedly—the way of resilience.

I find that certain components influence the building of this disposition we call resilience. To be able to manage our temperament, if you will, when the "heat" is on, we surrender to situations or conditions that activate 1) the exercise of faith, 2) the process of adapting, 3) the discipline of delayed gratification, and 4) the embracing of social responsibility. These components have helped me develop resiliency and both helped me as a father and as the President and CEO of The Piney Woods School, to provide opportunities for young people to develop resilience.

Faith

In its very nature, struggle commands our attention. As we tend to focus on the difficulties that block our goals, the stress of struggle tempts us into fear and defeat. Faith keeps us from succumbing to struggle because we do not focus on the problem or what we lack, but instead we see the possibilities on the other side of the struggle. When we confront fear with faith, we can see possibilities in the midst of our problems.

---

[65]   Viktor Frankl, *Man's Search for Meaning* (Boston: Beacon Press, 2006).

As a spiritual reality, faith is believing in something greater than oneself, such as our God. Faith likewise is also being persuaded of a tangible outcome, being convinced of a state or condition not presently visible. In this way, faith can be likened to confidence.

I barely remember elementary school. I remember certain episodes and some people, but I went to many different schools—changing schools seven times by the seventh grade—so none were truly impactful in my life. The church was. For much of my childhood, I was at church every Sunday, often from sunrise to sunset. I attended the Canaan "Baptist Church of Christ" and to this day remain confused about whether our denominational underpinnings were actually "Baptist" or more "Church of Christ." Our pastor, the Rev. Dr. Essex Elijah Franklin, took certain language quite literally. Rather than the more familiar "communion" of a wafer and grape juice served monthly on first Sundays, we celebrated the "Lord's Supper," and because no one eats supper in the morning, that service could take place only at 6 p.m. in the evening. Our family was always there. On third Sundays, we stayed late in the afternoon for Baptist Training Union. Add in Sunday School, one week revival services, children's choir rehearsals, vacation Bible school, and more. The consistent engagement of the church provided a stabilizing structure in my life, and without doubt, kept me off the streets of inner city, southside Chicago.

The real influence driving this relationship with the church was Big Momma, my maternal grandmother. I still think of her as Big Momma and had no idea that was not her actual name until someone at church kept calling her "Ms. Young." On days when my parents could not attend church, they always took us to service. Big Momma was there, and she would have it no other way. Because of Big Momma's influence and the imposing presence of church in our lives—enduring long hours of service, weekly, monthly, annually—I valued structure and developed an appreciation for the discipline that provides resilience.

Outwardly, I mastered these long, enduring stretches. Inwardly, my faith in God, the conviction that my existence was part of a bigger plan, and the certainty of His omnipresence and omnipotence became key building blocks for my life. This practice of enduring in the face of uncertainty for some greater purpose is itself a notable historical and cultural phenomenon within the Black community. As slaves, our forebears labored for the sake of freedom many of them never expected to personally realize, but they were nonetheless convinced their sacrifice would provide freedom to future generations. For me, such faithful endurance was further cultivated years later, in college.

After I graduated as valedictorian of my high school class, I attended the University of Chicago. My freshman year in college was one of transition, struggle, and fear. I moved from a small, predominantly Black, rural high school to a much larger, predominantly white, urban collegiate environment. Professor Edgar Epps, one of the few Black professors at that time, taught my core Humanities class. We read the great classics—authors like Homer, Socrates and Immanuel Kant—but unfortunately, these classics were unfamiliar to me, and my critical thinking skills were dormant. Partway through school, a close friend seemingly disappeared; I later discovered he had dropped out due to the rigors of the university.

I stayed because I had faith in God and faith that I would succeed. I did not remain in college because I was performing well. Initially, I was not. Nor did I remain because I knew what post-collegiate life held for me. I had no idea. My friend who had dropped out had attended a nationally top-ranked high school. I had not. There was no rational or logical reason for me to believe that I could compete at the university, except faith. Like enduring long services when I was child, I believed I had some greater purpose; I believed that God had some greater purpose for my life and my role—my responsibility—was to work earnestly in the present for the future that I could not fully see.

Unless we believe we can do something, we do not work to accomplish it. Our disposition—the choosing of our attitude in an unwelcome situation—yields a higher dividend than material profit. On the other side of struggle is an inner strength that cannot be removed. When we do not quit, we build the capacity to face the next crises.

Social Responsibility

Our faith in God matters, but so does the faith that others have in us. Often the faith we have in each other empowers us to persevere. As a recipient of such community empowerment, we inherit a social responsibility to be resilient. While I attended college, my "village" back down in Mississippi was rooting for my success. More than that, they expected me to succeed; they harbored no doubt about it. The students—my former schoolmates at Piney Woods—would send me care packages in which they had inserted short notes that communicated they were praying for me, counting on me, and believing in me. Alongside the power of my personal faith in God, the community's faith in my success established in me a social responsibility to overcome any challenge I would confront.

A variant of social responsibility includes generational impartation. Every generation has a baton to pass forward, but the next generation will not get the baton of resilience unless we prepare them to receive it. At Piney Woods, our next generation students develop resilience, that stick-to-itiveness that helps the Piney Woods family press through storms. Piney Woods' history is replete with such instances of resilience. In our earliest days, Laurence Clifton Jones taught poor Black students from the "schoolhouse" of no more than a fallen log. With no desks to be found, the earliest students used tree stumps as platforms for learning to write. An early visitor to this work, seeing everyone kneeling over these stumps, mistakenly thought she had interrupted our prayer time. When the school's only water tank needed repair, Jones, donning overalls like the male students, led the effort to fix it. Later, a tornado destroyed the wooden school building, In fact, at least six tornadoes have hit the Piney Woods campus since its founding in 1909. These repeated challenges, nurtured by faith in God and faith in the abilities of everyone there, have allowed seeds of resiliency to grow. With this approach to life, we echo Frankl's exhortation "to choose one's attitude in any given set of circumstances, to choose one's own way" and we exemplify one of my favorite Bible passages:

> *Not that I speak in respect of want: for I have learned,*
> *in whatsoever state I am, therewith to be content.*
> Philippians 4:11.

Our choice to be content despite adverse circumstances allows us to appreciate and work with what we have and innovate answers where seemingly none exist.

Adaptability

The message of Frankl's quote and the counsel of Hebrews 11:4 about the importance of faith are guides that help us adapt in our seasons of challenge. Instead of resisting challenge, which happens with discontentment, we view challenges as opportunities.

Adaptability is the ability to shift into new and different situations. To be adaptable, one must focus and see the good that an unwelcome condition offers. My dad suffered from an addiction to alcohol and eventually my parents separated. (Years later, my parents reunited and remain together today.) This brought on many moves and new schools, each with their share of challenges. My inability to escape these circumstances helped me learn to adapt. When my family lacked the resources to purchase bedroom furniture, I discovered that a nightstand and a shoe rack could be made from old plastic milk crates. I learned to use what we had, not dwell on what we lacked. In many instances, I was appreciative to have a bedroom at all. More often, when nighttime fell, the living room sofa functioned as my bed. At one time, we lived in a small basement cellar. My mother, cognizant that my three sisters and I were coming of age, divided the small area (which also housed the laundry area for the families that lived on the first and second floors of the duplex) with clotheslines hung with bedsheets. These were meant to give us a semblance of privacy or a "bedroom space." This component of resilience—adaptability—helps life become about purpose or usefulness, not materialism.

Delayed Gratification

Wonderful technological advances have compromised our capacity to wait. I confess I answer emails in the middle of the night, instead of waiting for a new workday to begin. During dinner at restaurants, we commonly observe children and parents alike sending direct messages or checking social media in the middle of the meal. The desire for instantaneous satisfaction makes us less resilient, and as a person who invests daily in future generation leaders, I believe the increasing expectation of instant satisfaction negatively impacts our children.

Our experience at Piney Woods, working to empower youth from across the globe, counsels that simply making our children wait may prove to be the most worthwhile gift we can provide them. Contemporary parents can take a lesson from my Big Momma: refuse to cave to kids' materialistic whims and refrain from immediate intervention as soon as things run south. By permitting kids to confront and respond to challenges, we develop within them endurance, perseverance, adaptability, and stronger faith.

One of my daughters took a good amount of cash to college, although my wife and I had covered all her expenses and shopped for any personal items or supplies she could possibly need. One month into the semester, she called me to ask for money to use an Uber to get back to her dorm. Her spending money was gone. Surprisingly to her, I said no, forcing her to use public transportation to get back to her dorm. She did not ask me for money again, and instead found a job. My daughter adapted to the lack of instant access to Mom and Dad's money. She became circumspect about how she spent the money she made. My refusal allowed her to realize the cost of instantaneous satisfaction and to develop the skill of prioritizing her wants. Too often we shield our children from a sense of being without. I suggest we consider taming the parental instinct for immediate intervention to protect our children from what they consider a difficult situation. Indeed, demonstrating deeper degrees of faith in our children's abilities to handle challenges will convey to them their social responsibility to be resilient.

Relatedly, delayed gratification implicates the power of prioritization: the ability to set two desires side by side and choose which one to put aside for a more opportune time. A student may say "I want to get a good grade in this class. I also want to go to the party, but my paper for this class is due." As they hone the ability to prioritize, they will begin to understand that once they get the good grade, they will be able to attend other parties. In this way, the practices of prioritization and delayed gratification offer them both rewards: a good paper and a good party.

At Piney Woods, we spend a lot of time helping learners develop these components of resilience. Delayed gratification promotes adaptability and faith. The component of resilience enhances decision-making skills and encourages prioritization. A young person must think through "What are the things that I really want versus the things that I need? Since I want to achieve this goal, these other things that I like need to wait." This deliberation is important for maturity and independence. We remind Piney Woods scholars regularly that freedom requires responsibility. In our campus lingo, we ask, "Of all the things I could do, what responsibly must I do?" The answer, and subsequent actions, often develop resilience.

Conclusion

The lessons I learned as a boy—at Piney Woods, in church, at home—all contribute to my ability to be resilient. Resilience brings a positive outcome, one that is largely internal, in which we relish accomplishing a difficult task or getting through a difficult season stronger than we were before.

In 2013, I was asked to join the Board of Piney Woods because the institution had struggled since the collapse of MCI WorldCom, to which prior Piney Woods trustees had tied a significant portion of the organization's endowed investments. While serving on the Board, I maintained my work in Washington, D.C. as a presidential appointee. When the head of Piney Woods decided to leave mid-year, the Board asked me to serve as interim president. I accepted, but the state of the school was on significantly unsteady ground.

Morale was low. Days before my arrival, the chief financial officer took another job. The student population had decreased. Buildings of more than a half-century old were literally falling down as roofs revealed substantial disrepair. We had no support staff. Conditions were dire. The Board questioned whether our time as an institution was over. These "storms" were clouding what was in the DNA of the institution: resilience.

Instead of focusing on the problem, I reminded the Board of our potential. One day, I walked the board members down to the pre-Civil War-era log cabin that had been donated as our first schoolhouse and boarding house. This is where our work began. I posed the question, "Why are we focused on what we have lost? Why not focus on what we have?" We had over twenty buildings and 2000 acres of land. My proposal was that if the Joneses could start with a dilapidated sheep shed—without heat, or air conditioning, or running water, or bathrooms—then we could take the legacy we inherited and get to the other side of these challenges. Ten years later, we remain in the fight to honor our legacy and restore this historic institution—the way of resilience.

The ability to get back up again after being knocked down, not to run from the stress of it but to choose one's attitude despite the situation—such skills are critical for every generation. At Piney Woods, I prepare our scholars: "There will be times in your life when things logically won't make sense, and you will wonder, 'Do I keep going?' The impetus to keep going is the realization that God does not call us to be successful; He calls us to be faithful."

6

THREE BLACK BARBERS WHO DID MUCH MORE THAN CUT HAIR

BY CYNTHIA MILLEN

Painstaking research into obscure old journals unearthed an amazing story of resilience—how thousands of slaves were saved by three men whose names to this day have almost been forgotten.

Stories are like wee stones you come upon when you are walking and somehow are drawn to stop and take a closer look. After sharper examination, you realize that the pebble you nearly stepped over contains a gem. Such was the case for me two years ago when I began research for a children's story.

I live in Northwest Ohio, the home of the deepest harbor (the Maumee River) for shipping on the Great Lakes, outstanding walleye fishing, the Toledo Mud Hens, Danny Thomas, Art Tatum, and especially for its extensive number of Underground Railroad safe houses. There are many which are identified by historical markers— houses, churches, barns, and various hideaways that were typically owned by well-known white abolitionists of the area. It is easy, and most obvious, to recognize these sites because they are real structures from a time when known people lived and had hiding places for others. There are streets (Winslow, Harroun, Lathrop) named for them, and public parks have often been created around these homes as a way to commemorate that time in our history. Ohio's history of "radical republicans" has been well-documented, and the author of the most famous depiction of slavery—Harriet Beecher Stowe, author of Uncle Tom's Cabin—lived and wrote her story from this state, so it was only logical that Northwest Ohio would play a part as well.

Similarly, the involvement of native tribes in assisting with hiding and ferrying runaway slaves in Ohio has long been studied. We know that Wyandot encampments on the Maumee River provided hiding spots for runaways, and that Ottawa tribesmen hid many slaves in the bottoms of their canoes as they carried them to freedom in Canada.

Finally, it has been long established that tens of thousands of runaway slaves came to and through Northwest Ohio, especially after the institution of the Fugitive Slave law in 1850, because this was the quickest way to Canada from any slave state. Previously, slaves considered themselves free once they crossed over into a free state. Through the passage of that infamous law, however, slaves were no longer safe, and those who hid them were in danger as well.

Bounty hunters now had great incentives, and assistance, to capture runaways. Hence, Canada was the only guarantee of freedom, and the shortest route in the United States was up the western edge of Ohio, often on the Miami-Erie Canal, to the Maumee River, and across Lake Erie to Amherstburg, Ontario. Unfortunately, those bounty hunters forced runaways to take more circuitous routes inland through swamp and forest away from the lake, making a quick journey much more arduous and dangerous. Thankfully, safe houses could be found all along the way, in rural Sylvania, Ohio; Lambertville, Michigan; Samaria, Michigan; and to Monroe, where a quick jaunt could be made up the shore and across the Detroit River to Ontario.

Ottawa tribesmen were especially helpful at this point because their tribes were permitted to flourish in Canada, even after they had been driven westward in the States. Documentation in Amherstburg, Ontario indicated that as many as sixty-thousand runaways came to its shores between 1850 and 1865. Although many settled in Canada after the war, many returned to the States to locate lost family members. A museum in Amherstburg documents their history and heartbreaking journeys.

Northwest Ohio was an especially treacherous place in the 1800s. It was the last area to be settled in Ohio due to its geography. The Black Swamp, as it is known, covered the area where Toledo currently lies. Walkways were frequently made out of wood and rope bridges elevated above the muck. Many people, especially Irish immigrants, were employed in dredging that muck to maintain the canals and river ways, and to create "plank" roads of wood for horses and carts to travel over the swamp. It was not uncommon for families to lose multiple children to cholera and malaria, diseases which flourished in the muggy area.

Maumee, to the south of Toledo, was just outside the swamp and had been established before Toledo. It was the end point of the Miami-Erie canal, and it was believed that it would soon be one of the major population centers of the U.S. The growth of the railroad, however, along with the draining of the swamp, allowed Toledo to take dominance in the area. By the time the Civil War ended, usage of the Miami-Erie canal had declined. Sylvania, to the west of Toledo, was named for its heavily forested landscape and is still one of the largest locations for the sandy Oak Openings ecosystems in the U.S. Though it took longer, it was much easier to travel around Toledo to Sylvania and into Michigan than to attempt a short cut through the great swamp.

As I delved deeper into my research, it occurred to me that while we could learn all about the safe houses and their owners, the contributions of various tribes, the routes and ultimate destination of the runaways, there was very little written about the operators themselves. Who coordinated the movement from one house to another? Who made the decision to take a group away from one route to a different one? How was the information shared about where the bounty hunters were or how many runaways needed to be hidden? How was all of this done for so many years and how did they keep it a secret?

Additionally, while it had been difficult to transport and hide runaways before the enactment of the Fugitive Slave law, how in the world had the operators managed to avoid the abusive penalties of this law? The 1850 act stipulated that persons aiding runaway slaves by providing food or shelter were subject to six months' imprisonment and $1,000 fines. Furthermore, it created a force of federal commissioners empowered to pursue fugitive slaves in any state and return them to their owners. It also required citizens to assist in the recovery of fugitive slaves, and it denied a fugitive's right to a jury trial. The act essentially forced citizens to assist in the recovery of escaped slaves, and if they were unwilling to assist, or aided a fugitive in escaping, they were subject to a fine and prosecution.

In the face of all of this, how were tens of thousands of runaway slaves transported to the Canadian border between 1850 and 1863, and by whom?

Thankfully, I found my answer in two places: an obscure article in the 1916 *Journal of Negro History* written by E. Delorus Preston, Jr. and a letter dated August 23, 1894. Entitled "The Underground Railroad in Northwest Ohio,"[66] the article written by Mr. Preston outlined the process on pages 432-433. Slaves were brought up to a center point in Findlay, Ohio, where a black barber named David Adams organized multiple parties in various safe houses to take them

---

[66] E. Delorus Preston, Jr., "The Underground Railroad in Northwest Ohio," *The Journal of Negro History, Volume 1, January 1916*, edited by Carter G. Woodson (CreateSpace Independent Publishing Platform, 2013), 432-433.

further north. Adam's father, also a barber, had long been involved in the Underground Railroad in Ohio, and his son continued the tradition. After leaving Findlay, the runaways were then taken in various groups over the thirty-six miles to Perrysburg, along the Maumee River or up the Miami-Erie canal, where another black barber met them. Then that unnamed Perrysburg barber arranged transport across the river to the Maumee/Toledo side where a third black barber, William Merritt, arranged transport to Canada—either by way of the river and across Lake Erie, or by a more circuitous and difficult inland route to Sylvania, into Michigan, and then over to Canada.

Without mentioning the barbers specifically, it was consistently noted in several other publications that not one of the thousands of runaways passing through northern Ohio was lost to bounty hunters.

The barbers had the advantage of serving all the white men in the area, so they were able to hear of any new arrivals. As members of the same profession, they were able to meet regularly and without suspicion to discuss plans and movements of people. As barbers, they could help to "clean up" and disguise the runaways coming in order to make their appearance less obvious, even dressing up men as women. Most importantly, as black men, they easily earned the trust of the runaways, who would obviously be hesitant to discuss their plight with a white man. But how did they keep their work secret?

David Adams' reputation in Findlay, Ohio, has been well established, but his relationship with the other two barbers was never discussed by him or his family during or immediately after the operation of the Railroad. It was only many years later that his descendants shared the information that his family always knew, by means of a detailed letter dictated by Mr. Adams on August 23, 1894:

> I would get a note to be sent south of Chamber
> Mills, 2 miles south of Findlay, to meet passen-
> gers. I never knew the parties or the conductors—

sometimes one, sometimes another—would bring the fugitives to the place agreed upon. At the edge of the woods, I'd find the passengers, and would run them out to old man King's (John King, a well-known abolitionist), 9 miles north, and leave them there 'til the next night, and then go and get them and take them on to Perrysburg, 36 miles. I used to deliver them to a barber in town, who turned them over to Wm. Merritt, on the other side of the Maumee River. Generally from there they were forwarded across the Michigan line. We used to take them different ways.

William Merritt, though he was well-known in the Toledo area for his eloquent involvement in voting rights conventions and especially for his avid advocacy of voting rights for women, kept his Underground Railroad activity secret. Though he and other black men would not earn the right to vote until 1870 in Ohio, he used his barber chair to successfully purchase a great deal of property in Toledo and establish himself as a highly respected businessman. At the time of his death, he was considered one of the wealthiest men in the area.

The existence of the third barber in Perrysburg, whose name to this day is still unknown and the coordinated relationship among the three men was never documented in print until Mr. Preston's article was published in 1916. Even William Siebert's authoritative history of the Underground Railroad,[67] published in 1898, did not mention the existence of the three barbers, but only noted Merritt in passing as one of several abolitionists in the area. Much more emphasis was placed upon the owners of the safe houses.

---

[67] William Siebert, *The Underground Railroad from Slavery to Freedom: A Comprehensive History* (New York: Macmillan, 1898).

In hindsight, it is clear the three barbers did everything in their power to hide their secret roles in bringing enslaved humans to freedom, and they did an excellent job. The fact that these men, with only rudimentary means of communication and transportation, were able to move tens of thousands of people successfully and secretly is nothing short of miraculous. These barbers, who themselves did not have rights equal to those of other men in Ohio, were able to successfully navigate past bounty hunters who often were sitting in their own barber chairs.

If only we could have been a fly on the wall in those three barbers' shops as they listened and drew out conversations that were helpful to their work! We will never know precisely how they passed information back and forth to one another or made their decisions regarding pathways and timing, but we do know they hid their precious cargo in barns, at the bottom of lumber wagons, underneath straw bales, and in mailing boxes. They did not lose even one runaway, and their secret work was never known during their lifetimes.

I hope that more is done to celebrate these gentle heroes and their brilliant bravery. I feel very blessed to have met their acquaintance, if only in the pages of old books.

7

FREDERICK MCKINLEY JONES

BY ROBERT L. WOODSON

"Fred never allowed the bigotry and prejudice of others to enter his heart or deter him from his insatiable desires to learn and to invent. Throughout his life, he seized every chance to hone his skills..."

Some years ago, I was impressed to hear the story of a black man who had invented the refrigeration system for trucks carrying perishable foodstuff. Then I learned that the same man also made trail-blazing contributions to the process that put sound to movies—as well as developing the portable X-ray unit, portable cooling units to preserve blood and medicines on the battlefield, and an entire spectrum of other critically important systems that have saved and improved lives. His name was Fred McKinley Jones, and his ground-breaking inventions were all around me. But why doesn't everyone know his name?

When I looked deeper into his background, I was even more impressed. I was searching for stories of resilience, and the story of this modest, unassuming man exemplified and even excelled much of what I have ever seen. Very few people, I believe, could survive the circumstances that characterized his early life, let alone accomplish such milestones in the arenas of innovation and invention.

Fred Jones was born in Covington, Kentucky, in 1893, to a black mother and Irish father at a time when interracial marriages were criminalized by most states. While he was just a baby, his mother deserted him, never to return. His father, John Jones, a railroad worker, was absent much of the time trying to earn a living. At seven, Fred was put in the care of a priest. Fred had no real benefit of parental presence. He was left to himself.

I was very moved by his story. I was the youngest of five children. My father died when I was nine, after a two-year hospitalization, leaving my mother—who had only a fifth-grade education—with four boys and a girl to raise. I experienced some of the same feelings of abandonment.

Emotional isolation causes a feeling that you don't deserve to have parenting, and you take steps to convince people you deserve to be loved. As time went on, Fred used his God-given talents to show he deserved to be accepted.

As a small child, he was shunned by the younger boys on his block and teased by the older ones who asked why his hair wasn't like theirs. He took to heart the one piece of advice his father gave him: "Don't pay a mind to what others say or the way they look at ya. Just go ahead and do what seems right for you!"

His unique character began to emerge, and one quality played a role in the resilience he had through life. He didn't dwell on what the other youths did or said, but pursued his passionate curiosity about the tools and objects in his world. To pass his time, young Fred pursued his fascination with investigating the way mechanisms functioned.

When Fred was just five years old, he successfully dismantled and reconstructed his father's broken watch. When he was six, the wheels of the makeshift wagon his father had built for him had worn to the rim, and his dad managed to save enough money to buy a small coaster wagon as a birthday gift. Fred was fascinated by how much easier the new model was to pull and took both wagons apart to discover the secret—a set of greasy ball bearings which he presented to his amazed father.

Neither Fred's school experience with rote learning, nor the mundane tasks that he was assigned while he was in the care of the priest, satisfied his passion for discovery and innovation.

He found some nourishment for his innate desire to learn about the way things work through a friendship he established with a man named Matthew, a chauffeur for a wealthy family. Matthew assigned Fred the task of keeping the household's two vehicles clean and polished, and he gladly accepted that responsibility.

One day, when Matthew had to take one of the vehicles to a garage in Cincinnati for repairs, he took ten-year-old Fred along with him. This was to become a turning point in Fred's life, as he intently watched every move of the mechanics and examined the fascinating array of tools, batteries, axles, and cars at Crothers' Garage.

Fred's desire to learn about machines became an obsession. At age eleven, still wearing knee pants, he slipped away from the rectory to make his way on his own. He headed to Crothers' Garage, confident that if he added a few years to his reported age, he would be hired at least to do some job. Fred eagerly accepted the task of cleaning up the floor and showed up three days early for his first day of work. He supplemented his earnings by working odd jobs in the evenings and saved enough to buy a pair of overalls.

Eventually Fred wrangled his way into doing some repairs and by the time he was fourteen, Mr. Crothers made him a full-time mechanic. Within three years, he became the foreman of the garage. As he availed himself of the repair manuals that were kept in the garage office, he continually expanded his knowledge of mechanics.

He gained enough expertise and skills to design racing cars—the "speed wagons" that were used to advertise Crothers' Garage at various races. When a racing team from the garage traveled to compete in an event but left Fred behind, he didn't stew in his situation but followed his conviction that it would only be fair that, as the designer of the race cars, he should be on-site to witness their performance. He left the garage against Mr. Crothers' orders and showed up at the race on his own.

Incensed by this breach of his orders, his employer announced that Fred would be on an "extended vacation" for an undetermined length of time. Rather than stay powerlessly idle until the end of his punishment, he quit his job as a foreman and hopped a freight train going South to seek new prospects as a mechanic.

Throughout that journey, he was rebuffed by garages whose owners told him, "Our customers wouldn't allow no colored boy working on their automobiles." Fred had no luck until he reached St. Louis and was hired to work in the boiler room of a steam-powered paddle boat. In time, impressed by Fred's ability to keep the steam pressure steady and even, the captain brought him up to the pilot house on top of the boat and introduced him to the river charts and maps needed to navigate the boat through the deepest and safest channels. When passengers occasionally objected to having a black in the pilot house and threatened to leave the boat, the captain invited them to do so.

Fred never allowed the bigotry and prejudice of others to enter his heart or deter him from his insatiable desire to learn and to invent. Throughout his life, he seized every chance to hone his skills, including registering for a mail-order course just to receive the reading material. His journey included repairing and improving farm machinery and modifying automobiles into race cars, including his famed Number 15 that he raced internationally.

At one point, Jones' emerging reputation as a "electrician" and "radioman" led to his meeting Joe Numero, a man who had established a reputation in the real-estate and manufacturing arenas. The friendship between the two developed into a partnership that delved into pioneering "talkies"— movies with sound.

Eventually, it led to leadership and dominance in the arena of refrigerated transport, which began with an incident in 1938. At that time, one of Numero's colleagues had lost an entire truckload of chickens that succumbed to the heat during travel. Fred, with his knack for turning problems into opportunities, was called to develop a solution. He went into action experimenting and within several weeks invented the refrigerated semi-truck. That accomplishment has since grown into the Thermo King Corporation, the renowned manufacturer of temperature-control systems used in refrigerator trucks and trailers; refrigerated railway cars and containers; and heating, ventilation and air-conditioning systems for bus and passenger rail vehicles. Today, Thermo King equipment is used in more than sixty countries with four hundred dealers throughout the world.

The refrigeration that Jones pioneered not only was a boon to the commercial food industry, but would later be invaluable throughout WWII, when a cooling system was vital to transporting temperature-sensitive medication and blood plasma to American soldiers abroad.

Jones' inventions would also include a lightweight radio that was a precursor to the transistor—a milestone in communication—as well as the prototype of a snowmobile, which he created from skis mounted to the undercarriage of an old airplane body that was attached to an airplane motor and propellor. Jones created this vehicle to facilitate the life-salvaging work of the doctors whom he transported in the course of his career. He then focused his mind, expertise, and inventiveness to produce a portable x-ray machine that doctors could use at their patients' homes.

One key to Jones' trailblazing engineering prowess was his ability to recognize opportunities for combining different mechanisms and materials—building new mechanisms from everything from parts of his previous inventions to objects he discovered in a scrap yard. In sum, Fred had 20-20 insight and assumed that others should have the same visionary capacity.

Despite the great engineering strides Jones made, monetary rewards were never his priority. He received a salary, bonuses, a place to live, and the fringe benefits that Thermo King offered to all its employees, and he never wanted more. In fact, he often dispersed whatever money he had in his pocket to workers at the plant who were in need.

Throughout his fantastic life journey, Fred single-mindedly pursued the goals of invention and discovery without giving weight to the racism and bigotry that surrounded him since childhood. Later in life, he gave no notice to the fact that Numero would have to reserve a room for his "anonymous guest" at a white-only hotel where they would meet with business prospects. He maintained this same immunity from resentment even when he was invited to participate in meetings in Washington with the Department of Defense to discuss what equipment would be best for the army to use—but could not stay in the same hotels as the other engineers because he was black.

In 1952, his advice to young people at a ceremony where he was presented with an award for his "outstanding achievements that serve as an inspiration to youth" crossed all boundaries of race and ethnicity. "Don't be afraid to get your hands dirty. Don't be afraid of work. Try many jobs," he declared, adding, "You have to read. Find out what others know. Believe in yourself. If you think you are right about something, don't listen to others tell you you're wrong. Remember, nothing is impossible. Go ahead and prove you're right."

In 1961, Fred Jones succumbed to lung cancer at the age of sixty-eight, leaving behind a legacy of inventions that would have worldwide impact as well as a long list of awards and honors.

Among them, in 1944, Jones became the first African American to become a member of the American Society of Refrigeration

Engineers. In 1953, he received the Merit Award of the Phyllis Wheatley Auxiliary for the inspiration he provided for young people. He was posthumously inducted to the Minnesota Inventors Hall of Fame in 1977 and the National Inventors Hall of Fame in 2007. In 1991, the National Medal of Technology was posthumously awarded to Joseph A. Numero and Frederick M. Jones by President George Bush. In 1996, the Thermo King Model C refrigeration unit—the world's first front-mount refrigeration unit for mobile trucks—was designated an International Mechanical Engineering Landmark by the American Society of Mechanical Engineers.

During his lifetime, Jones accumulated more than sixty patents, forty of which were related to refrigeration. His impressive cutting-edge inventions and contributions to society are even more awe-inspiring when appreciated in the context of his life and times and the daunting challenges he faced.[68]

As in my case, the name Fred McKinley Jones may not have been familiar to you. But if items in your grocery cart recently included a frozen pizza or a carton of ice cream, you've felt the impact of his innovative mind—the creation of the first refrigerated unit for a semi-trailer truck. In addition, if you've recently viewed the latest blockbuster movie, you may give a hat tip to Jones, who made trail-blazing strides in the creation of "talkie" films, syncing sound to moving pictures. And, if you were sitting in an air-conditioned theater, once again, you can thank Fred Jones.

Fred McKinley Jones demonstrates how the human spirit can overcome the absence of parenting and the absence of someone who mentored him or championed his cause. Perhaps not one in ten thousand people could overcome the challenges he faced.

Throughout history, the principles of self-determination and personal responsibility not only have empowered men and women with

---

[68] Virginia Ott and Gloria Swanson, *Man with a Million Ideas.* (Minneapolis: Lerner Publications Company, 1977).

the resilience to succeed in spite of daunting odds, but also to leave legacies that would benefit others—both in their time and for centuries to come. Such is the case of the inspiring life and awe-inspiring accomplishments of Frederick McKinley Jones.

8

THE RESILIENCE OF TV RESPECTABILITY

BY YAYA JATA FANUSIE

The artistic resilience of The Cosby Show *is
revealed when it is watched today—still. It shows
a universe that beckons us to be the best of ourselves.
The Huxtable world is a cherished ideal that demonstrates how to be an excellent human being, even
when our reality is a world where human beings
can easily fall into the lowest depths of the low.*

I magine a television show where the showrunners make a con-
certed effort to infuse the entire program with a very specific
social agenda—so much so that they hire an outside expert who
is ignorant about screenwriting and show business, but who specializes in a particular set of social issues. They ask him to review every
single episode's script before it goes into production and to even
influence the casting of guest actors. No episode gets released if it
strays from a clearly orchestrated message and the show producer's
social sensibilities.

This is not hard to imagine. In fact, it sounds like the formula
of much of Hollywood's current programming, where cultural and

political agendas don't just seep into shows. They submerge them. There's a prevailing sentiment among growing audiences that television has gone too "woke" and that heavy-handed social agendas are ruining entertainment, or at the very least, narrowing Hollywood's scope of appeal. The term "go woke, go broke" has been circulating for years, somewhat in jest, but in 2024 it is becoming a pretty reliable observation.[69] Thinly veiled social messaging in TV and film is often not resonating.[70]

But the show that I'm discussing did not go broke. It did not alienate viewers, although it certainly had an agenda. It entertained the nation. In fact, it did its job so well that it became the highest rated situation comedy of all time. That program was *The Cosby Show*.

The Cosby Show broke ground, not just because it was an all-African-American sitcom that stayed as the number one show in America for five straight seasons. It did something no other hit show starring African Americans had done (and I would say, few have been able to do ever since): *The Cosby Show* promoted a high, universal human ideal in a black family context, and through that mode, won popular and critical approval.

The Cosby Show is a prime example of resilience in the African American cultural arts experience. Before its premiere, racism and bigotry had maligned the public image of blacks for decades in Hollywood. Even though earlier black shows in the 1970s became bona fide hits, they often trafficked in stereotypes around African American poverty and family strife. So, it is remarkable that one of the most successful sitcoms of all-time actually portrayed black

---

[69] Aleks Phillips, "Go Woke, Go Broke? Millennials Say It's True," *Newsweek*, May 19, 2023, https://www.newsweek.com/millennials-most-likely-support-go-woke-go-broke-poll-1801438.

[70] Caroline Frost, "'Is TV Too Woke?': Industry & Media Debate Buzz Topic & Reveal Eye-Opening Survey On Disparity Between Public & TV Sector Views—Edinburgh," *Deadline*, August 25, 2021, https://deadline.com/2021/08/tv-too-woke-the-office-it-crowd-edinburgh-1234821978/.

excellence, featuring an upwardly mobile, loving African American couple, both alumni from HBCUs, who formed a family that stayed intact across three generations. Their children, despite various ups and downs, pursued higher education and worked to be productive members of society.

This sitcom, created by Bill Cosby about an upper-middle-class African American family living in Brooklyn, NY, aired from 1984 to 1992 with a key goal: to entertain families in a way that would be healthy for all children,[71] but especially black children. The focus was not so much about a singular message. Rather, it was about having the best psychological impact on its viewers.

This agenda was not secret at all. It was reported on widely during the show's early success. What has rarely been unpacked is how the show accomplished its goal subtly without preaching, but with tact and wisdom that appears lost on the cultural architects of Hollywood who have followed in its wake.[72]

Recoding Blackness

When Bill Cosby began to plan for *The Cosby Show*, he turned to Dr. Alvin Poussaint,[73] a Harlem-born psychiatrist with a strong

---

[71] Lindsey E. Mccormack, "Professor Shaped Eight Years Of 'Cosby'," *Harvard Crimson*, May 24, 2002, https://www.thecrimson.com/article/2002/5/24/professor-shaped-eight-years-of-cosby/.

[72] An exception is a 2003 Lehigh University Master's Thesis by Anson Ferguson, whose paper, "The Cosby Show and Its Role in Breaking Stereotypes" provides a great treatment of the show's focus on education and positive role models and discusses criticisms around the show's overwhelmingly positive portrayals. [Anson Ferguson, "The Cosby Show and Its Role in Breaking Stereotypes" (MA thesis, Lehigh University, 2003), https://preserve.lib.lehigh.edu/islandora/object/preserve:bp-3101395.]

[73] Harvard Medical School, "Alvin F. Poussaint, MD," https://meded.hms.harvard.edu/people/alvin-poussaint-md.

pedigree[74] in the civil rights movement, to consult on the content of the program. Poussaint's academic and clinical expertise was on child development, family health, and violence. He was hired to help ensure that the episodes showed dynamics that would convey values that would support a child's healthy psychological growth and stay away from ideas or depictions that would be harmful for childhood development. Priorities were to show loving marriage relationships, nurturing parent-child interactions, and to not inculcate bad behaviors and stereotypes.

The last priority was the one which Hollywood did the worst in during the decades prior. The television show *Good Times* was a major hit, but focused on a poor black family living in Chicago's Cabrini Green projects. The oldest son character, J.J. Evans—who evolved into the show's main star—was viewed as a buffoon[75] by many, including John Amos, the actor who played the father of the household, and whom the writers eventually wrote off in a car accident after Amos continuously voiced anger[76] over the way the writers were over-emphasizing JJ's "jive" character-type. And so, *Good Times* soon became like the shows *What's Happening* and *That's My Mama!* that centered on families with no fathers in the home.

The main characters in *Sanford and Son* were junkmen. And in *The Jeffersons*, George and Louise were a rags-to-riches African American couple unexpectedly thrust into New York wealth. But George remained a trash-talking verbal bully who didn't get much real respect from others, not even from his own maid.

---

74   Alvin F. Poussaint, video interview series, The National Visionary Leadership Project (NVLP), updated April 23, 2014, https://www.youtube.com/playlist?list=P LCwE4GdJdVRIzXpbja7H-8E3gs5E0ati3.

75   Joshua Hammer, "Must Blacks Be Buffoons?", *Newsweek*, October 25, 1992, https://www.newsweek.com/must-blacks-be-buffoons-200088.

76   Okla Jones, "Throwback Thursday Interview: John Amos Reveals How Departure From 'Good Times' Went Down," *Essence*, August 12, 2021, https://www.essence.com/entertainment/throwback-thursday-interview-john-amos-reveals-how-departure-from-good-times-went-down/.

In *Diff'rent Strokes* and *Webster*, the starring black boy characters were orphans (with physical growth deficiencies) who had to be
saved by the upper-class Caucasians who adopted them. To grossly
paraphrase the late comedian Robin Harris, it seems quite odd that
there were no African American relatives who could have taken in
those children.

So, *The Cosby Show* was crafted to present a strong family unit
in the form of the Huxtables. This did not mean the family lacked
conflict. The children regularly were at odds with each other or with
Mom and Dad (especially Dad), but conflict was always resolved
respectfully. The parents, Cliff and Clair, had plenty of disagree-
ments, but never resorted to traumatizing fights, shouting matches, or
undignified insults. Both pairs of grandparents were married and had
good relationships with their grandchildren.

The show's team made sure the nuclear family was modeled upon
high standards of conduct. The central character was Bill Cosby's
role of Cliff. He was the show's comedic anchor, a playful father who
could be the butt of a joke, but never a clown. He was respected by
family members, but not feared as a tyrant. He had a high-powered
career as a physician, but did not take himself too seriously, nor was
he intimidated by his wife's similar career success as a New York City
lawyer. The couple had a strong marriage with no signs of infidelity
or distrust, and they kept their romantic spark alive. They were living
an enviable and prosperous upper middle-class life in 1980s America.

A longstanding criticism of *The Cosby Show* in some black intellectual circles[77] has been that its perceived strength of the African
American family it portrayed was actually a weakness, because it
was supposedly unrealistic. It did not portray the undeniable ele-

---

[77] Chauncey Devega, "How 'The Cosby Show' Duped America: The sitcom that
enabled our ugliest Reagan-era fantasies," *Salon*, July 12, 2015, https://www.
salon.com/2015/07/12/how_the_cosby_show_duped_america_the_sitcom_that_
enabled_our_ugliest_reagan_era_fantasies/.

ments of racism and discrimination that these characters likely would
have faced in the real world. It stayed away from hot-button social
or political issues of its time, although it referenced the civil rights
movement nostalgically. Critics lamented that the show seemed to
ignore much of what may have been problematic around U.S. racial
relations. The Huxtables certainly didn't talk much about race, to the
chagrin of some real-life black intelligentsia. There was an assumption that their blackness was not authentic. There were even arguments in the 1980s that unironically accused the show of the sin of
presenting that blacks were "just like" white people.[78]

What is odd is that the critics seemed to not understand Cosby's
and Poussaint's strategic wisdom in building the Huxtable universe in
such a manner. In one interview (referenced in Anson Ferguson's MA
thesis[79]), Poussaint explained that "critical social disorders, like racism, violence, and drug abuse, rarely lend themselves to comic treatment; trying to deal with them on a sitcom could trivialize issues that
deserve serious, thoughtful treatment."

But it is not accurate to say that *The Cosby Show* never showed
the racism and discrimination that its upper middle class African
American family would face in "real life." It was simply judicious
in treating those topics and did so without expanding microaggres-
sions into personal catastrophes for the characters. For example, in
the Season 5 episode, "Mrs. Huxtable Goes to Kindergarten,"[80] Clair
finds herself as the only African American (and woman) on a local
TV talk show panel. Within the first few minutes of the panel

---

[78] Henry Louis Gates Jr., "TV's Black World Turns - But Stays Unreal," *New York Times*, November 12, 1989, https://www.nytimes.com/1989/11/12/arts/tv-s-black-world-turns-but-stays-unreal.html.

[79] Ferguson, "The Cosby Show and Its Role in Breaking Stereotypes." *https://core.ac.uk/download/pdf/228643994.pdf*

[80] *The Cosby Show*, season 5, episode 13, "Mrs. Huxtable Goes to Kindergarten," directed by Carl Lauten and Chuck Vinson, written by Ed Weinberger, Michael Leeson, and Bill Cosby, aired January 26, 1989, https://www.imdb.com/title/tt0547033/.

discussion, it becomes clear that the other panelists—all white men—are rude and dismissive. They view her as less intellectually capable and expect her to only comment on "black" topics. Interestingly, the men include both liberal and conservative thinkers. Clair deals with their ignorance and racism with dignity and class. The title of the episode actually implies the childishness of the men's behavior, showing that a mature response would be to not give such behavior much oxygen. At the episode's end, Clair is offered a permanent role on the talk show because of her great contribution, but she turns it down, explaining that she feels no need to try to prove herself to anybody. It is a nuanced example of resiliency. Subtle racism was countered, well, subtly.

The Cosby Show did deal head-on with sensitive social topics like drug and alcohol abuse, and even teen pregnancy. However, the storylines always revolved around friends caught up in those predicaments, not the main characters. For example, in one episode the Huxtable parents found a marijuana joint in their son Theo's schoolbook. However, it belonged not to him, but to a friend. When teenage pregnancy was discussed, it was not due to a predicament of one of the Huxtable girls, but a friend of second-oldest daughter Denise. And when such topics were woven into the storylines, they were some of the show's most dramatic moments, giving the topics the gravity they deserved in a 1980s environment where such issues were becoming national concerns. In such episodes, the Huxtable parents were counseling and comforting forces for the guest characters who faced these crises.

It's noteworthy that Bill Cosby has a doctorate in education[81] (as does his wife Camille, who is a longtime advocate for African

---

[81]   Ana Figueroa, "Cost and Effect," *AARP*, June 8, 2006, https://www.aarp.org/personal-growth/life-stories/info-2006/billcosby.html

American education[82]). He and Poussaint stressed the pursuit of education as a recurring theme of *The Cosby Show* and constructed storylines with a no-excuses approach to social and educational advancement for children. Interestingly, most cultural commentators who wrote loudly about wanting the program to show more "realistic" depictions of race and society did not have degrees in child education or child psychology. Even though some critics argue that the Huxtable universe was a fantasy of fiction, there seems to be little peer-reviewed educational research indicating that children would be better served in their psychological growth by being infused with heavy TV content about racism, violence, and family strife. And one might wonder what sort of ideals and images these same intellectuals promote in their own households. Do they incline personally toward *The Cosby Show*'s Cliff Huxtable or those of *Good Times*' J.J. Evans? It's quite likely that they push for Huxtable principles in their own homes, but I digress.

Those lambasting *The Cosby Show*'s supposed lack of realism simply do not get the program's purposeful methodology for educating and uplifting families and children. As one description of the show's behind-the-scenes efforts put it, Alvin Poussaint was hired to "recode blackness" to a high moral standard vision of African American possibility, where blacks could be perceived in all types of stories and circumstances—just like white people.

Accusing *The Cosby Show* of black inauthenticity is a much flimsier argument after four decades of hindsight. The series presented the true experiences, successes, and culture of middle-class African American families to the nation, a feat not previously accomplished. No TV family did more to popularize HBCUs than the Huxtables,

---

82   Manuel Roig-Franzia, "Camille Cosby: A life spent juggling her role as public figure with desire to stay private," *Washington Post*, December 23, 2014, https://www.washingtonpost.com/lifestyle/style/camille-cosby-a-life-spent-juggling-her-role-as-public-figure-with-desire-to-be-private/2014/12/23/575ad31e-8528-11e4-9534-f79a23c40e6c_story.html.

as evidenced by the show's spinoff *A Different World* that took place in Cliff and Clair's fictional alma mater of Hillman College, modeled after the colleges of Hampton, Howard, Morehouse and Spellman. And *The Cosby Show* was the first program to consistently and strategically place African American cultural artifacts into the background of each show. Sometimes, black art would move to the foreground like the episode in Season 2 where Clair pays $11,000 at an auction for a famous painting by African American artist Ellis Wilson.[83] The show had a constant stream of guest appearances by countless African American musicians, singers, and actors who brought the wealth of black cultural achievement up close into America's living rooms. Every Thursday night, *The Cosby Show* exposed people of all cultural backgrounds to the beauty of the black experience. Viewers likely learned more about African American culture and history on *The Cosby Show* than they did watching *The Jeffersons* or *Good Times*. It probably did more to improve race relations and counter bigotry and bias toward African Americans than any show since, reaching millions of households who had no intimate connections with African American families in real life.

The Universal Soul, Presented in the African American Milieu

The Cosby Show's unique accomplishment was to envelop storylines around African American life in a way that attracted and interested everybody. It became such a hit because the family interactions were relatable—beyond race, age, and even class. Although the majority of households do not have parents who are well-off doctors and lawyers, everyone in most homes can relate on some level to bickering over

---

[83]   *The Cosby Show*, season 2, episode 13, "The Auction," directed by Jay Sandrich, written by Ed Weinberger, Michael Leeson, and Bill Cosby, aired January 9, 1986, https://www.imdb.com/title/tt0547070/.

things like grades, clothing choices, chores, or curfews. The Huxtables episodes hinged on these mundane interactions, driven by family storylines—not punchlines.

This was not accidental. The executive producers of the show (who happened to be Caucasian) said in interviews that when they approached Bill Cosby, they were motivated by a standup routine he had given on NBC in the early 1980s. In Cosby's repertoire going back decades, his humor never hinged on jokes relating to race, but to the everyday predicaments of families of any color. Cosby approached comedy this way even though he was active in promoting black social upliftment in other non-comedic media campaigns[84] in the 1960s.

The Cosby Show from its inception walked a fine line between being a family show and being a black family show. By emphasizing universal storylines, it became the first black show to not be just a black show. While other sitcoms were usually written as black characters in "black" circumstances, with universal comedic themes layered on top of them, *The Cosby Show* was written as a universally relatable family at its core, with African American culture and themes layered on top of it.

But *The Cosby Show* formula must not have been formulaic enough. It was a unique creation. There certainly was a rise of black sitcom content in the 1990s (probably thanks to *The Cosby Show's* high ratings), but *The Fresh Prince of Bel Air*, *Roc*, *Living Single*, *Martin*, *Moesha*, *The Jamie Foxx Show* and *Hangin' with Mr. Cooper*, although commercially successful, never duplicated its massive appeal for the entire nation. What was its secret? It should be pointed out that none of those other sitcoms focused singularly on a traditional nuclear family unit. The one show which might have tried the hardest at being like *The Cosby Show* was *Family Matters*, which started in

---

[84] "Black History: Lost, Stolen or Strayed (1968)," Reelblack One, posted on YouTube April 6, 2018, https://www.youtube.com/watch?v=QXn-Fm6cn9s&ab_channel=ReelblackOne.

1989. All this shows how compelling the Huxtables were as human characters, not just cultural ones. Their souls were written as human, not black. And through this approach, the show elevated the public consciousness around African American people.

Fathers' Day

In aiming to convey themes to support the best psychological development of children, especially black children, *The Cosby Show* excelled in a key area: advancing positive portrayals of men, especially in fatherhood. Typically, the father was absent in African American-majority sitcoms. When he was present, he might have been realistic in some ways and even relatable in the black culture context, but not an ideal role model from a child psychology standpoint. A good example is James Evans, the patriarch in *Good Times*. He was a strong working man, committed to supporting his family. But his quick resorting to belt discipline was a pretty common comedic theme that could never be written for a Cliff Huxtable. That would never have made it past Dr. Poussaint.

Cliff Huxtable superseded previous versions of men, especially black men because of his fullness as a character. Cliff's occupation was important, but it did not drive the show's universe, as did Andy Griffith's sheriff character in *The Andy Griffith Show*. Cliff was a father of five, but also a very present son to his senior-citizen dad. The show delved into his pastimes, idiosyncrasies, and backstory, such as his wannabe repairman tendencies, his preferences for hoagies and all tasty, but unhealthy food and his nostalgia for his college days running track and field.

Compare that multifacetedness to the one-dimensional George Jefferson—known mostly for his ability to quip, argue, and insult. Or, to the title African American character in *Benson* who rose from butler to lieutenant governor, but the audience learned very little about his personal background or anything outside of his daily work. In fact, the whole premise of *Benson* revolved around him successfully managing the affairs of everyone (who happened to be white) in the governor's mansion. If Benson ever had a romantic interest in the show, it was a rare occurrence.

Television fathers might not ever be like Cliff Huxtable again. *The Cosby Show* premiered at a time when family sitcoms actually were in decline. It revived them for a while. But the TV fatherhood in the decades since has returned to typically unenviable characters. Today, Homer Simpson is a more likely television model for a family dad than Cliff Huxtable. Fathers remain on shows, but there do not appear to be producers and writers asking the question, "What type of father is ideal for a child's best psychological development?"

Times have changed. In fact, referring to a universal or ideal nuclear family is triggering for many people. The Critical Race Theory aspersions toward the so-called patriarchy that were present mostly in niche university circles during the 1980s, are now the embedded default position in most institutions of mainstream media and entertainment. So, it is unlikely in the current cultural climate for a Cliff Huxtable to be regarded as an ideal when the most influential culture-creators would argue that in fact there is no ideal. All measures of what it means to be a father, or even a man, are subjective, thus unmeasurable. A "good father" is now in the eye of the screenwriter, without any larger objective or moral reference.

And television itself is no longer the great cultural unifier. *The Cosby Show* began when there were only three television networks and less than half of American homes[85] had cable. *The Cosby Show* formula of targeting universal appeal was built for that time. TV today is on demand, literally and figuratively: streaming enabling viewers

---

[85] Brad Adgate, "The Rise And Fall Of Cable Television," *Forbes*, November 2, 2020, https://www.forbes.com/sites/bradadgate/2020/11/02/the-rise-and-fall-of-cable-television/?sh=297d41d26b31.

to watch whenever they wish, and for streaming sites to craft shows catering to anyone. Human souls have a universal core, but there are countless identities that media platforms now can cater to.

The Cosby Show's Asterisk

A tragedy of *The Cosby Show*'s representation of African American resilience is that its legacy will always be tainted by Bill Cosby's sexual crimes against women. This writer believes it is possible to separate the art of the show—and what went into its creation—from the despicable longstanding private, but now publicly known, behavior of the man behind it. In fact, it is necessary to be able to distinguish between them; if we review cultural art with a litmus test of the personal behavior of its creator away from his or her work, we will not really be judging the art itself.

This does not mean that Bill Cosby's activities and their impact should not be addressed when thinking about *The Cosby Show*'s legacy. Many have written about this, but it may be most appropriate to reference the words of Kierna Mayo, former Editor-in-Chief of *Ebony Magazine* who wrote in 2018:[86]

> I know that beautiful Black men like my father, who do not abuse, exist across generations and have through every era of American life. Therefore, I refuse to have my passion and pride for the creative genius and iconography of The Cosby Show allow me to be the slightest bit confused. I don't have to ride for the fallen, decrepit Bill Cosby to prove what I know about Black excellence, Black decency, Black humor, Black art,

---

[86] Kierna Mayo, "Bill Cosby and Our Reality of a Shattered Black 'Hero'," *Afropunk*, October 3, 2018, https://afropunk.com/2018/10/bill-cosby-and-our-shattered-black-hero/.

Black colleges, Black family, Black mothers—or
Black male heroes.

Bill Cosby's tragic flaws and his fallen stature reinforce the point that Cliff Huxtable and the Huxtable family actually reflected a moral model. That model was in service to the viewers, especially to the children who were in deep need for fulsome, affirming examples of healthy family life. The artistic resilience of *The Cosby Show* is still evident when it is watched today, because it shows a universe that beckons us to be our best selves. The Huxtable world is a cherished ideal that demonstrates how to be an excellent human being, even when our reality is a world where human beings can easily fall into the lowest depths of the low.

PART II:
THE EVIDENCE

I

FROM CRACK HOUSE TO LIFE HOUSE—THE NORTH HILL COMMUNITY CENTER

BY GARY AND PATRICIA WYATT

Every grassroots organization will face the unbelief of naysayers, the red tape of city policies, and complaints from those they serve. Mistakes will even be made, but these setbacks can turn into comebacks if quitting or adjusting the core mission to appease other people is not an option.

Whether a single mother starts her own business, a child masters a difficult level in a video game, or a young man sells drugs to gang members, resilience—working hard in a particular direction under challenging circumstances—is at play. Resilience is a mindset with corresponding action that influences both immediate and long-term outcomes. That woman makes her first sale, the child's mastery takes him to the next level, and the young man either pockets a wad of hundred-dollar bills or gets caught in the act and spends the rest of his young life in prison. In other words, a person's priorities or life direction at any given moment dictate where their resilience is going to show up.

As elementary school students in Akron, Ohio, we had no idea we would get involved with selling cocaine and then later become mentors and ministers to that same crowd. God loves to make broken people whole again. Our individual struggles and the choices that came out of those struggles catapulted us into this endeavor to turn an Akron, Ohio crack house into a life house that we named the North Hill Community House.

Building a vision, in our case a non-profit, is not easy. The failure rate is high. To persist takes a vision larger and purer than any human being can invent, because success in this work—helping thugs, prostitutes, homeless people, and impoverished families with their practical needs—shatters the hopes of money in the bank, a continuous brigade of volunteers, or a compartmentalized work-family dynamic. In addition, as the mission grows, so does the pressure, because people end up relying on these organizations. Grassroots leaders must stay grounded and humble as their vision goes from a simple operation to a full-blown enterprise that bears fruit.

The vision that God gave us unfolded in stages. After running Toys for Tots from our car, we began operating from the basement of our house, which was in the same south Akron neighborhood where Gary had sold and used crack cocaine. Then in 2004, God gave us the vision to move and set up a community house—a place where residents of all ages could gather and receive practical support—on the north side of Akron on Howard Street, which had a horrible reputation in the 1980s and 1990s, being the main location for illegal activity and violence.

A relative owned a house on Howard Street that we rented, and we began to gameplan our ministry strategies. A quick walk from our rental was a large multi-residence home that had been used for drugs, prostitution, and even dogfighting. At one time, Gary's oldest brother would get high in this house. God told us that this was where we would set up camp. His plan was to turn a crack house into a life house, to redeem a street just like He redeemed me and my husband. In 2007, we got a mortgage on this house.

While the space and the location were a dream come true, the ninety-year-old house was a wreck. The outside had been spray-painted with graffiti and the basement drain was broken. The first thing we did was buy paint, but it took years of sweat equity (we had no money) and donated materials and furniture to get the place in a workable condition. I tell people who want advice: work hard, do not complain, and do not worry about the process of building a vision. When an opportunity arises, complaining about what the opportunity looks like is not an option. Purchasing that house was the first step in helping the neighborhood experience a comeback. Both Gary and I worked full-time, raised our boys, worked the ministry, and the pace was tiring. But the passion we had for the community gave us the joy and the strength to press on, every day.

The house itself is not the ministry—we would have served any-where—but the house is a symbol. Just as Gary went from crack to Christ, so in a sense did the house. No longer tattered and torn, a place of crime and addiction, it is inviting and colorful and has become a place of refuge. This house is now a feeding facility, a tutor-ing facility, a learning facility—a happy facility. When God tells you where to plant your stake in the ground, He will help you bloom from where you are planted.

Sometimes resilience shows up by looking at the small amount of food in the refrigerator and splitting it up so everyone has at least one bite to eat. If the power bill goes unpaid and the electricity is turned off, the resilient put kids in the same bed and pile on the blan-kets. The poor, the traumatized, and even the homeless will figure out something to make life work, even if it is using a dirty trash bag as a cover from the rain. Poor and wounded people do what they have to do to get by and survive. We let them know that they can bounce back from every setback. Our staffers and volunteers praise residents for their effort and encourage them to keep moving forward little by little. The road to transformation for a person or a neighborhood is never peaches and cream. The good thing about struggle—the pressure of a tough life—is that it shapes us.

The Covid-19 pandemic was a struggle as well as a motivator. Despite working full-time jobs, we had to keep the food pantry running since the other 416 food bank sites in the greater Akron area temporarily shut down—their volunteers were older and the risk of Covid was greater. Eventually, our food pantry was declared an emergency site for Akron. Ironically, Covid-19 was not a triggering issue for the impoverished residents in our area who were used to dealing with more days in the month than money in the bank. These residents withstood the challenge of lack better than those in our nation who were used to having their cabinets filled. Although we were never afraid of Covid-19, we took wise precautions so that everyone could stay safe and healthy. Sometimes, many of the volunteers did not show up, but we stayed open. The shelves in the stores could not stay stocked and the elderly were not getting there fast enough to get what they needed, and since they wanted to protect themselves from the virus, we started delivering food to them. The pandemic caused us to rise to another level of service. We did not shut down and not one of us caught Covid-19 during that process.

When you do this type of ministry and you do have a family, your children become an extension of the work. Include family members, even children, in the work, but also make sure that their family-time needs are met. We have Black sons that we have to prepare for the world, and in doing so we must develop their resilience when they have issues at school, on the playground or at their first job. Kids must learn to bounce back too. They also must learn to serve; for example, as a teenager, one of our sons started taking extra food with him to work because he knew that occasionally one of his friends would show up hungry.

As for overall family relationships, kids are not always aware of the struggles in their parents' marriage, but they need to learn how to withstand the pressures of life that impact all relationships. Our boys know our story, our troubles and how we worked on our relationship. Any couple that decides to pursue this mission together needs to stay conscious of their personal issues and work on their marriage as much as they work in the community. Listening to each other, honesty, not airing personal laundry in public, and genuine friendship is important for organizational and marital longevity. It can take decades to smooth out the rough spots in a marriage. However, those being served do not expect perfection, they want authenticity. In fact, when people understand the toil and perseverance that community leaders experience in their own lives, they will no longer run away from hard situations by using drugs or the like, but they will be encouraged to face difficult situations and overcome, no matter how long it takes.

Our boys have known us as Dad and Mom, but also as father and mother figures to many other kids. Understanding the dynamics of being a good parent and mothering and fathering the children in the community is vital. North Hill Community House serves children who live in stressful home environments, often being raised by one adult, a grandparent or their mother.

The lessons I (Patricia) teach my sons are the same life skills that I teach my students in our tutoring programs. Two important life skills are choosing good companions and making quality choices. I focus on these topics because many of the students we serve often acquiesce to the "no snitching" culture, not understanding that the word "snitch" started in the prison system. Because of this "no snitching" culture, these young people will see bad things happen to others in and out of school, or even experience trauma themselves and not tell anybody. The need for belonging and acceptance often makes them compliant, and natural models for healthy relationships are not around them. So kids will choose to stay silent, believing they are protecting a friend, when they need to cry for help, knowing that safety and protection for themselves and others comes with openness. Men and women who do this type of work need to help these young people understand that healthy friendships, marriages, and family relationships require a transparency that prevents many types of abuse, neglect, and crime.

Another level of pressure comes with increasing organizational success. At one time, supporters encouraged us to move our organization into larger buildings that were outside of our neighborhood. We said no; community-minded leaders must stay true to their core mission. North Hill Community House is a *neighborhood* oasis; it will remain a "mom and pop" style organization. Residents are grateful when community-based entities remain where the need is. It is crucial to resist the temptations that come with large-scale attention if they steer you from your core mission. Every grassroots organization will face the unbelief of naysayers, the red tape of city policies, and complaints from those they serve. Mistakes will even be made, but these setbacks can turn into comebacks if quitting or adjusting the core mission to appease other people is not an option.

The core of our grassroots mission is community revitalization by educating, empowering, and equipping the people in our community to develop productive lives that allow them to make a difference. We would not be able to do this work with excellence without exceptional forerunners and role models. Going from crack to Christ put me (Gary) in the path of Bob Woodson. Getting to know him was a divine encounter for me, because I had never met a national figure doing great things in communities across the country. His message is one of overcoming. Bob's mentorship, and the mission of the Woodson Center, compels Patricia and me to do our part where we have been planted. Besides Bob and Community Affiliate Network (CAN) members being part of our village, so are various pastors, educators, and professional people. These provide an iron-sharpens-iron benefit for us. All grassroots leaders need sharp people in their village, people who inspire, have different giftings, offer wisdom and direction, or personal counseling and professional expertise.

God is the beginning, the end, and the center of why we do what we do. Since we grew up in poverty, we understand financial struggle. Instead of turning our backs on the people, we live among the people. Helping people comprehend His love in big ways and small ways is the least we can do. Of course, we cannot take away people's pain or immediately change their circumstances, but we can encourage that single mother who has to go right back home into a hard situation. We can supply her with food and tutor her kids. We can reach out to the whole family—the children, the mother, the daddy, the grandmother or aunt—so we can help everybody in any way we can. A bad choice never has to be the conclusion to someone's story. In fact, Jesus Himself turned what appeared like a setback—being crucified on the Cross—into the greatest comeback in history.

In 2008, when the economy was at its worst and the housing market was suffering, we bought and renovated a dilapidated house with a bad history, but over time built a prosperous place of community life and hope. God's story through us reveals that when resilience, vision, and hard work are in the mix, a crippled community can become a beacon of life.

2

THE WILL TO LIVE WITH PURPOSE

BY SYLVIA BENNETT-STONE,
VOICES OF BLACK MOTHERS UNITED

We must embrace resilience when emotion is high.
We must embrace resilience when injustice continues.
Resilience is pushing past the shock and horror of the
crime. The resilient resist knee-jerk reactions and
then they coordinate a solution-oriented response.

H uman beings are uncomfortable facing someone else's pain. People often switch television channels when a newscast features poverty in Third World countries or shows the devastation of a natural disaster. Some gloss over news stories about children killed in a crossfire. Others may skim over a social media post about the college student from Silicon Valley who committed suicide, or the young woman who died from an opioid overdose.

Desensitizing is a form of pain-avoidance, especially these days when tragedy and chaos seem constant. It also is an impediment that faces organizations like the Voices of Black Mothers United as we go about our mission to heal both individuals and communities. Some readers may have already felt tempted to turn from these pages, preferring a lighter topic.

The Voices of Black Mothers United (VBMU) seeks to help society understand the pain endured by mothers who have lost their children to violence, and to recognize that 1) if these mothers do not heal, the family and the community will not heal, 2) action is needed to lower the rate of homicides in our communities, and 3) unaddressed trauma leads to mental health issues, substance abuse, and further violence in our communities. We all must take intentional actions for a positive change.

My daughter, Krystal Joy, was shot while she and her friend were in their car at a gas station. One bullet, two deaths. Thousands of residents in Alabama were shocked when Krystal's murderer was proclaimed not guilty and set free. After the verdict, shots were fired at our house for about a week. Although I, my husband, and our son were victimized, many residents in our city experienced the emotional impact of the crime and the unjust trial, and then became concerned about their own safety.

As human beings, we should have an emotional response to someone's pain. But violent retaliation worsens the situation and compounds the stress that a community already feels. We must embrace resilience when emotion is high. We must embrace resilience when injustice continues. Resilience is pushing past the shock and horror of the crime. The resilient resist knee-jerk reactions and recognize the immediate needs of the family first. Then they coordinate a solution-oriented response.

VBMU helps communities set aside vigilante-style justice and embrace a level of resilience that honors the grieving mothers of the slain, allowing them to take the lead and be the voice of protests that include solutions.

When a homicide is widely publicized, I advise the mother to communicate her desires to the community. Her voice must be heard

saying, "Stand down, community. Follow my lead. That was my child."
No mother wants another mother to lose their child because somebody, somewhere, wants to avenge the death through violent retaliation. The mothers of the slain must lead the way to closure, which
includes turning the tragedy into a triumph.

VBMU's most notable outcomes involve mothers who not only
forgave their child's murderers but went to the prisons to pray for
them. We have even had mothers of the victims reach out to the
mothers of the criminals. Such actions are an overwhelming display
of overcoming adversity.

The anti-police rhetoric in the last few years fuels already frail
emotions in the Black community. Contrary to media opinion,
Black communities want a police presence in their midst. "Defund
the police" is not a welcome mantra among 80 percent of the Black
population. Unfortunately, this statistic is rarely broadcast. Distress
in the Black community exists not because of police officers shooting
Blacks; but because of the epidemic of Black-on-Black crime.

My daughter and her friend were caught in a crossfire initiated by
two Black men, not white police officers. Media refuses to highlight
this problem. But many Black-led community-based organizations
like VBMU recognize this. The enemy of the innocent usually has
the same skin color as they do.

VBMU works with the police, firmly believing they are vital
to the security of our crime-ridden communities. Yet we promote
accountability and antidiscrimination initiatives in police departments. We want our police officers to be what their oath requires:
"keep the peace" officers.

The trauma of this epidemic—gang wars, gun violence, other
fatal crimes—takes a toll most of the public does not understand.
The goal of our information campaigns is to inform neighborhood
residents so they not only become safe havens for the hurting, but
proactive neighbors who can identify risk factors that could cause

another homicide. Most of these criminals come from low-income, single-parent families, and many have unaddressed childhood trauma. What we must do is link arms and provide sufficient support and resources for the entire community. VBMU engages with local leaders and pastors to raise awareness about mental health needs and innovate organic solutions from those most affected by the violence: the residents. One of our mission statements is "A safe neighborhood starts with YOU taking action."

When a fatality occurs, one resident may die, but many are victims, because pain is like a tornado that builds or shifts according to internal or external forces, and it causes destruction wherever it travels. It is important to realize that any neighborhood may have as many as five mothers on one street who have lost a child to violence. One street! Multiply this and you have a community that copes with the violent event by becoming numb, in denial, hopeless, or enraged. Some will want to retaliate against the offenders or their families. The dysfunction on that block is chaotic because you have various expressions of the grieving process occurring and coming not only from the mothers, but their family members and others in the community.

With the suddenness of the death, any immediate publicity or violence in the aftermath impacts and scars the entire family. The remaining kids might start acting out; the spouse or significant other might start drinking. As those family relationships tailspin and deteriorate any semblance of security, the wounded state of the family persists because those around them feel unequipped—they do not know how to offer solace. Their coping methods or maladaptive behaviors are visible to neighbors, church or club members, and even employers, if that mother cannot get out of bed to go to work.

More Americans must join the movement against community violence and controversial laws that deny victims true justice. We can become advocates for the grieving mother and then be responsible problem-solvers in our communities. Where homicides have occurred, VBMU seeks to implement and maintain a constant presence in that area—whether a street or a section of a city—for a period of time, to meet mothers where they are. The cycle of community deterioration can be stopped, but it begins with the mothers. If the mother does not heal, no one heals.

As grief counselors—specifically Victims Service Advocates certified through the Department of Justice Office of Victims Services—being resilient keeps the leaders of VMBU in the fight to help mothers, families, and communities overcome. Every day, we say "yes" to the call despite the emotional toll.

A few years ago, on July 4th, an eight-year-old little boy was caught in a crossfire shooting inside a very busy shopping mall in Birmingham Alabama. The same day, I received the call about my daughter Krystal. Of course, this really struck a chord because it was the Fourth of July. The bullet hit him in the head, and he instantly died on site as everyone watched. This mother was doubly devastated, as was I, to hear about this kind of violence in a public mall. I immediately rushed to aid this very young mother to help her digest watching her baby die. Along with many community members, I was very vocal in expressing our opinions regarding the senseless violence. Meanwhile, others asked us to silence our thoughts because it was diluting the message of the very few police shootings of blacks. While silence was not an option, I had to maintain my composure as well as be the voice of reason and guidance, to positively lead the community to avoid destructive rhetoric or retaliations, so we could focus on the issues at hand. It's been an extremely long road for this mother, but to date she is doing better.

Low-income communities across the nation deal with fatal violence way too much—many times multiple homicides in one day. These deaths shatter every mother's heart and the community's peace of mind, exacerbating preexisting feelings of injustice and hopelessness. As Director of VBMU, when I meet a mom whose pain is fresh,

I still feel that momentary twinge of pain of my own loss. "I know exactly how you are feeling right now" is the first thing I say to grieving black mothers. Then as a grief advocate counselor, I must press through the personal triggers I experience, and focus on the cries and groans of another shellshocked mother. For me, resilience is the will to keep living and fighting through this very painful reality while the world keeps on turning. It's the will to find what's your new normal and how to balance such pain. It's finding the way of letting go the anger while finding a way to be a good person.

Sometimes I must sit still for a minute after I end a phone call where I have had to talk to a mother dealing with suicidal ideation. Often these women hurt so badly that death seems like their only escape from the pain. Fighting for someone who is unable to fight for themselves is a passion that requires wisdom, persistence, and patience—all components of resilience. My ability to remain calm and composed in these desperate minutes is a sign to me that God's strength and ability is present, because the pain and hopelessness I hear from my fellow sisters would break most people. In addition, there are just some things that can only be shared with someone who's walked that walk—someone who knows exactly what you are experiencing.

Fox News once invited me and another mother-survivor of this type of loss onto their newscast. Before the production, I heard the other mother who was to be interviewed make a comment about committing suicide. Automatically, I went from Sylvia the person, to Sylvia the advocate. I told everyone to leave the lounge so I could help her, because twenty-six percent of parents die within the first ten years of losing a child to homicide.

Another devastating outcome, besides suicidal ideation, is when the pain produces self-sabotaging behavior or mental health issues like depression. Depression has a voracious appetite: in time, it takes its toll on your body as well as your mind. Depression not only affects you, but its tentacles reach out, squeezing the joy out of everyone in its path. Depression, simply put, is being in a state of disease in the mind. The state of your mind affects your physical body. I became ill, had shortness of breath, elevated blood pressure, and tightening in my chest. I found myself being admitted to the hospital for angioplasty surgery.

Depression can creep in any time after a child's death, but especially when isolation sets in. A mother often feels alone because in a widely publicized homicide, the public focuses on marches, violent protests, the failures of the court system, or issues with law enforcement. Moreover, publicized or not, at some point neighbors, school peers, and co-workers eventually go on with their lives. Close friends or relatives may not visit as much, because the mother's emotional state becomes too much for them to deal with. These are difficult times for a mother, when people tiptoe around because they really do not know what to say or how to bring her comfort and closure.

Recovery can happen, but it takes time and oftentimes professional assistance. The Black community must stop not only stigmatizing mental health issues, but also being in denial when someone in our family has a mental health challenge. If we identify mental health issues in our lives or among family members, and get the necessary help, we can possibly prevent a homicide or a suicide.

My pain did not kill me but propelled me to purpose—pushing through the pain of my own loss to help fellow moms and communities recover from the devastation caused by these untimely deaths. Through the Voices of Black Mothers United, I counsel grieving mothers, promote positive policing initiatives and other community partnerships, and help the leaders of our state chapters demonstrate how the power of forgiveness and resilience saves future lives.

Black women are not the only women to experience the trauma of losing a child to violence. In our Mothers Consortium, we had mothers of every skin-color and socioeconomic status attend. Our goal is to be present in every state, because when it comes to losing a child to a violent crime, our pain is the same. The *God's Word* translation of Jeremiah 29:11 says, "I know the plans that I have for you, declares the LORD. They are plans for peace and not disaster, plans to give you a future filled with hope." This road to this promised future requires resilience. Every time another child is killed, we push harder. We do more.

3

REFRAMING BROKEN LIVES

BY RON ANDERSON,
PROJECT RECLAIM

*As community-based leaders, we must help at-risk
youth and the parent or grandparent raising them
recognize the resiliency that lies within. Resilience
is the ability to withstand life's turbulence, the
ability to overcome obstacles that appear out of
nowhere. It is part of the DNA of our human spirit.*

Violent deaths occur regularly in low-income communities, and instinctively residents brace themselves every day for the reality of a possible drug overdose, an episode of gun and gang violence, or a case of domestic abuse in their neighborhood, or even within their homes. Sadly, some teachers have no idea how often students who live in high crime communities show up struggling internally because of what they have experienced at home or in the streets.

Resilience often seems dormant or nonexistent in those who are strung out, skipping school, or goofing off in class. Labeled by many as "bad" or "thugs," these at-risk youth are too often forsaken. In addition, a reciprocal dynamic develops within their communities: the unfavorable environment influences their actions, and their actions exacerbate the environment.

No matter what the misfortune—death, abandonment, poverty—young and old alike can feel isolated and believe no one knows what they are going through or can identify with their adverse experience. When situations at home or in the community impact them in deleterious and negative ways, eventually they entertain certain subconscious thoughts: *There must be something wrong with me because so many bad things are going on around me.* I call this impression "singularity." This perception of aloneness creates an incubator of silent emotions that will produce an array of maladaptive behaviors. Fortunately, this cancer is treatable, and the treatment begins with an innate desire to live. To thrive. To know the world and be known, accepted, and part of its success.

In high school, I grievously injured a fellow student. The boy was rushed to the emergency room, and the principal told me that if I did not pay the boy's medical bill, I would be expelled and not allowed to attend any school in the parish. Needing help, I went to my step-father's mother, because I didn't have anyone to go to at home. She said to me, "I know what you want. You want me to pay that boy's doctor bill." I said, "Yes ma'am." She said, "Well, I tell you what, I've already paid it. But I'll be damned if I pay another one. And if you don't get yourself together and get straightened up, I'm gonna have you taken away and put in a boy's home or a detention center somewhere, 'cause I'm tired of you." Her response pushed me into the next pivotal conversation.

Ms. June Turner was our high school guidance counselor. While she listened to me relate to her what I was going through, she went to her file cabinet and pulled out my academic record. Looking it over, she commented that my grades were fine until a certain time. She said, "Tell me what happened."

"Tell me what happened." Fireworks went off in my brain. All that time, with everything that was going on around me, I thought I was the problem. But Ms. Turner illustrated to me that it wasn't me by explaining, "You're not a bad child—you're an angry child." Her explanation hit the nail on the head. I had seen a brutal attempted murder when I was eight years old, and over time, the overwhelming memory caused me to become violent.

Social predictors placed me in the category of "Black boys who die in the streets or end up in prison." These predictions, well-known by those they identify, become a stigma, a stain, a scarlet letter of sorts that Black boys may embrace. Their self-concept is further skewed because school administrators sometimes misdiagnose symptoms of trauma—learning disabilities for example—and the root cause of cognitive challenges remains unaddressed. Educational, social services, and mental health spheres are necessary partners in a young person's recovery, but they may not adequately determine a person's outcome. I will not bend my knee to these prognostications because I am a witness that with the right guidance, the human spirit will overcome.

So what do we do about the teenager who seems to ignore the road to improvement? They keep getting in trouble, acting out from unhealed wounds, or they regularly make self-sabotaging choices. We must become their mentors—visionaries to show them what they have not seen. Reframing their story is the beginning. My re-formation started my junior year in high school when Ms. Turner helped me reframe my troubled mind.

As community-based leaders, we must help at-risk youth and the parent or grandparent raising them recognize the resiliency that lies within. Resilience is the ability to withstand life's turbulence, the ability to overcome obstacles that appear out of nowhere. It is part of the DNA of our human spirit. While resilience can be seen outwardly—through physical action—it begins with an attitude which, when kindled, helps people dismiss hopelessness and embrace agency. It would be a great disservice for people to keep thinking they are weak, when in fact, they are strong. The sentiment of the revered spiritual "We Shall Overcome" reflects the resilience of a troubled people facing troubling times. When I point out to parents or their children that they are resilient, that they are strong, I get leverage to help them reframe many of their perceptions. Singularity loses.

We must tell people that if they are still in the struggle, they have not given up! Parents who are still hoping and praying for their kids have not given up. The teens who get out of bed and go to school—despite not having food to eat—have not given up! In the Black community, we have a phrase, "going through it," which expresses a mentality that life's struggles are inevitable and uncontrollable. In this mindset, people view themselves as living martyrs of Fate. To destroy the subconscious acquiescence to this fatalistic perspective, we must help people admit that their spirit is still in the game—the core of their humanity is still striving for abundant life. *They have not given up!*

Project Reclaim helps youth and their parents attain their potential. We identify their pain point and capitalize on their desire to be pain-free. For example, one high school student, Stephanie (not her real name), refused to do any work although she came to school every day—often to escape the troubles at home. The hidden pain showed up one day in a life skills class. I had asked the students to name their heroes. Most mentioned a parent, grandparent, or another relative. I heard Stephanie say, "I'm so tired of hearing them talk about their mothers and fathers!" Usually, to be expedient, someone in my position would have reprimanded a student who was speaking out of turn and disrupting the class. But I caught the pain that caused her response. Stephanie was communicating something. Her counselors later divulged that when she was young, she witnessed her father murder her mother. So, I enrolled her in our program. Unprompted, she wrote an article for our last newsletter:

Mr. Anderson talked to us about him coming from where he came from, what he had to go through, and where he is now. To me that message meant if he can do that and come from all that, so can I...My past doesn't define me. What I went through will not hold me back from what I need to do for myself.

Through a myriad of classes and workshops, Project Reclaim has seen excellent results helping hundreds of young people reframe their story by 1) identifying their present obstacles, 2) improving their self-concept, 3) becoming self-confident, and 4) contributing to their communities.

Our main goals are to reduce teenage pregnancies and juvenile offenses and help students matriculate into high school, college, or a vocational or technical school. We also teach life skills to help youth stay away from the drug culture and limit negative media and pop culture influence. We offer a framework of constant affirmation and high expectations.

We are living in a new era with new challenges. New levels of disrespect challenge community leaders like me who have done this work for over three decades. In addition, many of today's youth are hyperviolent. I am enrolling ten-year-olds in the program, not just for shoplifting at the local Walmart, but because they are using weapons in their neighborhoods. In our town of about 13,000 residents, we've had as many shootings per capita as the largest cities. A shooting occurred recently about three miles from my home. The kids needing mentorship are younger and their disposition makes them harder to reach. Trust is anathema to them.

My style has changed in teaching juvenile offenders in our life skills classes. Sometimes I must be more direct, more forceful in my approach, without disrespecting them. Gone are the days when in the first session I would crank up a PowerPoint to discuss optimal potential and the concept of excellence and goal setting. Implementing novel approaches must become more comfortable for us now. One day, I began with, "We're doing this program to keep your 'so-and-so' out of prison." And I told them the reality of their situation— where they were headed if they did not change. This approach gets the attention of this new generation. I stay respectful because it is counterproductive to meet hostility with hostility. I have the authority in that room; I do not abuse that authority.

The mental and emotional stress of the work is constant, and because of this we need relationships with others in the grassroots community. This can be very lonely work, so hearing from people around the country who face the same challenges and are in the same fight is vital to our own wellbeing. Singularity can strike the most seasoned community organizers, but when we hear from others who fight the same battles, we sigh and think, *I'm not the only one seeing this.*

Resiliency is stoked when people, like those of the Woodson Center, come alongside and stimulate fresh vision and spark new ideas. The Center's Community Affiliate Network (CAN) offers cathartic and thought-provoking opportunities to engage with others who do this work.

On one call, the term "institutional narcissism" was mentioned. This occurs when agencies, foundations, or other service organizations believe they have all the answers that a community needs but have not actually walked on the streets of the neighborhoods or visited the programs offered by grassroots organizations like ours. This issue, stated openly among a peer group of community-based organizers, magnified the importance of community ownership and indigenous, organic solutions.

Identifying residents that have a gift for leadership and a passion for the community will help maintain the momentum of transforming our communities. In our communities are visionaries, those whose rhetoric will move people to action and those who can identify and obtain resources. Contrary to the ideas hashed out in a board-room, homegrown solutions from those who live in poverty, witness violence, and see the outcomes will prove that the most the outside "experts" can do is speculate and theorize.

Years ago, I decided it would be more effective for a parent to lead our parent group instead of me, believing that peer-to-peer relation-ships would create a team concept for parents, rather than an auto-cratic leadership model. One mom accepted the role and innovated the theme PACT, which stands for Parents and Children Together. As a collective, they work to raise their kids together and are involved in Project Reclaim, which instills camaraderie, mutual support, and encouragement for parents and children alike.

When parents reach out to other parents, when kids serve as ambassadors and reach out to other kids, they are doing more than promoting a program, they are calling out potential. Peer engagement is a shield against singularity and a rich resource for innovation.

One new initiative for PACT will be "Going Through It To-gether," and the first topic we will discuss is resilience. Most parents we encounter are grateful for this program and willing to be involved. Their partnership is vital. It shows that as a community, although we are buffeted by the vagaries of life and things that we encounter, no matter what we are faced with, no matter how difficult life is, we can get through this. Struggle builds resilience.

Some of the parents arrive at our program combative and defen-sive. Perhaps their children were ordered by the court to enroll, or their child's grades are poor. I let them know we are not going to criticize them and that as a certified parenting instructor, I have strat-egies to offer that may help them raise their kids. As soon as their defenses come down, we can discuss rules, limits, effective techniques for praise and encouragement and behavioral traps like rewarding with money. Eventually parents grow more at ease. Our desire is not only to give them some victories in their role as parents but also to demonstrate a victorious mentality. My heart's desire is to communicate this message to parents:

> *You possess strength you don't see. You are dealing with issues other people can't handle because they haven't developed the same strengths. Because you've grown up in the circumstances that you have, you've had to find a way to make ends meet, to raise your kids, to discover resources that will help you and your children. You have recognized the need and resolved to address the need. This is a display of resilience. This shows that you have reflected on your life and circumstance. Stay the course! Keep your strength!*

In school, we learned that success is conditional, not guaranteed. If a young person's past can be reframed as a launch pad, then they will leap forward and not stay trapped by their circumstances. Anyone can thrive, no matter how traumatic their beginning. If we communicate the innate fortitude of the human spirit, if we reframe a person's outlook, if we exchange the narrative of defeat for evidence of triumph, then our work will be successful.

American history is replete with examples of enduring hope and accomplished vision. Martin Luther King, Jr., Medgar Evers, and my cousin Fred Hampton are three. My uncle J.D. Hampton was the first Black man to run for mayor here in Minden, Louisiana. Although he didn't win, the victory for him was that more black people registered to vote at that time than any time in the history of the parish. This is an accomplishment. This is radical grace: others before self. The civil rights movement was about people who had a will to release change. They willed themselves through adversity and as a result, the people who were not born yet—you and I—have reaped the benefits.

The challenges within low-income communities can be overcome if we put our will to it. We were created to withstand storms and grow through pressure. If life knocks us down, we rise. Black history proves this. American history proves this. We have the capacity, we have the resources, and within the community, we have the manpower. So, transformation is a matter of our wills. *Will we do it?*

4

NATURE VS. NURTURE: EVERYTHING IS POSSIBLE

BY SHEENA MICHELE MASON, PH.D.

*In my most depressive and down times, I
reminded myself that there was more to life than
those times and that those times fortified me
into one unstoppable and exceptional force.*

O ver the years, I have often asked myself how I've come to
be me. In primary school, I distinctly remember learning
about the nature versus nurture debate among psychologists. *Nature* refers to how genetics influence an individual's personality and development. In contrast, *nurture* refers to how their
environment, including relationships and experiences, impacts their
development. Psychologists still debate whether nature or nurture
plays a more significant role in how we become who we are. While I
haven't come down firmly on either side of the debate, I have come to
see my personality and development primarily as the result of nurture
and persistent faith in a higher power and a higher purpose.

Paradoxically, the idea of *nurture* leading to my success implies
that I likely had a carefree childhood with little adversity between
now and then. But to say that I have overcome tremendous adversity

would be to understate what I endured and overcame. I want to shine a light on how knowing that everything is possible, even in the darkest times, and my willingness to question everything, especially myself, has enabled me to overcome tremendous trauma.

To my knowledge, my biological father finished high school or the equivalent and joined the military. He rests in a military cemetery. My biological mother never finished high school and has some intellectual disability. I was taken from their custody at birth since two biological brothers died under suspicious circumstances, and authorities found two of my biological sisters severely neglected while in their care. Tommy and Virgil—my brothers—were less than three months old when they passed. My sisters, Yvonne and Geneva, were under eight years old. The cruel irony is that while my sisters were adopted and raised together in a nurturing—though imperfect—home, I was adopted by a different family where I suffered severe abuse at the hands of my adoptive mother and neglect by both adoptive parents.

Once, when I was nine or ten, I ran away to a friend's house. My adoptive father found me and returned me to the trailer they called home. If looks could have killed me, my adoptive mother would have succeeded in taking my life that night. The police came. At first, I refused to talk about what had been done to me, but after they started to leave me there, I disclosed it, naively believing they would shepherd me to safety. Instead, they just told me I should call them if she did it again and asked if I knew how to contact them.

After the sheriffs left, my adoptive parents burst through my bedroom door with black trash bags. They put all my clothes and stuffed animals into the bags. My adoptive mother shouted about how I was not getting anything back until the end of summer and the start of the new school year. She said that I would get one of my adoptive father's shirts and a clean pair of underwear to use each day and that I could only leave my room to clean the entire house, which I did every day. Before falling asleep, I saw a stray belt that did not fit into a bag on my bedroom floor. I thought to hide it but foolishly left it there, falling asleep completely dejected.

I woke to her beating me with the belt. She discarded the belt and hit me with my alarm clock, swinging it by its cord. She left and went to work. Upon her return, she came into my room and told me to sit on my floor with my feet flat on the ground, knees to my chest, and arms raised straight in front of me. I knew she would break my fingers or exert much effort trying. I was confused about adding my feet, which was not part of the regularly scheduled program.

She raised her hand that held a wooden spoon above and behind her head, bringing it down with all her force onto my outstretched fingers. She kept hollering to raise my arms back up after she smashed my hands with the spoon. After what felt like forever, she did the same to my feet and toes. She explained that she had "saved" me from my adoptive father's wrath, and she would do that to my hands and feet every day for the next two weeks as payback.

She delivered on her promise for a few days. On something like day four or five, I tiptoed to the living room where she sat watching TV and begged her for mercy with tears streaming down my face. She never made eye contact with me. That was the first and only time I ever dared to stand up for myself to her brutality. I threw all fear of reprisal out of the window. If she was going to kill me, I was ready. But I was not going to keep enduring that for another week plus. She never responded verbally to my pleas. But she did not return the next day to do the same thing. My body was finally able to start healing until her next beating. She could not break me emotionally and spiritually, either. For as long as I can remember, I immersed myself in school, music, sports, and God.

I read voraciously. While my "family" was poor, we lived near a more affluent community. That meant I had access to any book I wanted to read, via a public library, so I did. By the time I turned twelve, I had read every book for my age group and transitioned to adult books. Dean Koontz and Stephen King were two of my favorite writers. I remember liking their books because of how weighty they felt in my hands. There were so many pages to explore. My most prized possessions were an encyclopedia collection and every *Goosebumps* book. If you wanted to hurt me, destroy one of my books, or keep me away from books altogether.

To my knowledge, my adoptive parents finished high school. My adoptive father joined the Navy and after serving, became a correctional officer. My adoptive mother had immigrated to the United States from Panama in her early twenties and worked at a pharmaceutical factory. They didn't do much by way of encouraging my love of reading and school, but they also didn't get in my way. I thought earning straight As and being a "perfect" student would earn my adoptive mother's love. I was wrong. But a result of my belief was that I thrived in school, my primary safe place. Teachers loved me, and I adored them.

I'll never forget when Miss Morris, my second-grade teacher, got down to eye level with me, put her hands on my shoulders, and just looked at me. I don't remember what she said or if she said anything. I remember that I felt seen that day—I felt valued. I suspect that she was the one who called Child Protective Services (CPS) that school year. CPS failed in its duty to protect me. But my belief that Miss Morris was someone who sensed my abuse and did the right thing by trying to help me gave me inner strength and perseverance for the rest of my primary school experiences. It took that one person to believe in me. Or, at least, it took me thinking that one person believed in me and saw me as a whole person outside of what I was experiencing, to help me along the way.

When I was a senior in high school, I had to drop out of school. I was an AP and honors student taking college Economics and English courses, a varsity athlete, and a selective choir and band member. But

I had chosen homelessness over staying in that personal hell. As a result, I had "bigger fish to fry" and couldn't stay in high school for my last year.

Kathy Frasier, my social worker at school, was the second person I met during my childhood and teenage years who had an everlasting impact on me. When my Economics and English teachers understandably expressed fear that I would become a statistic and not finish high school, Ms. Frasier looked into my eyes. She said, "I know that Sheena will finish and go on to college as she plans. It's just a matter of when."

I always knew that God meant more for my life than what I was experiencing. Literature, and more broadly, education, were gateways to my faith in God's greater purpose for me. I accessed worlds I could only imagine through literature and education and found connections with characters and historical figures. These connections fostered my increasingly firm belief in the possibility of everything. While I could've just as easily "become a statistic," I believed in myself. As they say, I knew I was meant to turn my mess into a message. Everything I went through and overcame was so that I could be a mirror for others in the face of adversity to know that they, too, could overcome everything.

After I dropped out of high school, I found my way back the next school year and finished at the top of my class. I went on to graduate, finishing again at the top of my class and being the student commencement speaker. I endured more heartache and trauma during my undergraduate studies and after graduation. I lived through it all, from persistent homelessness to domestic violence and food scarcity, to getting hit by a city bus while walking across the street. I maintained that everything was possible and that I was meant for more. I didn't know what the more would be. Still, I knew it involved earning a Ph.D. and helping people, both through academia and education, and in what I call the "real world" outside of academia.

During my journey toward fulfilling my purpose, I worked my way up the corporate ladder, was a Teach For America corps member, lived in five different states on different coasts, traveled internationally, graduated in the top 1 percent of my MA program at the University of Houston, and graduated again at the top of the class at Howard University, where I was again chosen as a student commencement speaker. I passed "with distinction," an honor reserved for less than 1 percent of humanities Ph.Ds. worldwide. Before I graduated with my Ph.D. in May 2022, I had secured my first book contract with an academic press for a refined version of my dissertation.

I started as an Assistant Professor in the Fall of 2022. I secured a second book contract before the end of the school year. I will refrain from listing every other notable accomplishment. Long story short, I've done a lot in a brief timeframe, and continue to do a lot. Why? I know that my life's purpose requires me to be the best version of myself. Everything is possible, especially when people try to put limitations on me being me. I'm willing to question everything, including myself, which has continued to be to my benefit and exponential growth. I always remain in a growth mindset.

My growth mindset enabled me to stop trying to be "perfect" to earn anyone else's love and to start striving to be the best possible version of myself—always for myself—and to fulfill God's purpose for me. Now, I admit I don't have a traditional view of religion. While I grew up Roman Catholic, I've since expanded my thoughts about God, theology and spirituality. But my belief in a higher power, a greater purpose, remains. My love for reading and learning and my access to a decent education and any book I wanted empowered me to bear witness to more than I had the context to believe. I saw myself operating within a much bigger context my human mind couldn't understand or ultimately know. Yet, I knew that my part was greater than my limited frame of reference. And it was my sustained belief in a higher power and greater purpose that held my entire knowledge system together. Two well-timed adults who expressed confidence in me in different ways also helped me get through some of the darkest times.

In my most depressive and down times, I reminded myself that there was more to life than those times and that those times fortified me into one unstoppable and exceptional force.

Others, one would expect, like family, didn't exactly nurture me during vital years. Circumstances forced me to nurture and nourish myself—a tall order for any young person or child. Fairness wasn't part of the equation. Be that as it may, the confluence of the events and beliefs I named—and any part nature plays—didn't just sustain me but helped me not just to survive and thrive, but to kick down mountains and take names. I'll likely always wonder how I've come to be me in the face of such adversity. Yet, I think I know intuitively, as I've outlined here. In all, I think that had any spoke of the wheels been missing or damaged, I wouldn't be me, just as I sincerely doubt that I wouldn't be me had I not gone through everything I did.

My path has been challenging. But I'm here, still standing tall and with much to share with anyone who listens.

5

MY JOURNEY FROM THE DEPTHS OF HOMELESSNESS TO THE HEIGHTS OF FLIGHT

BY KAMIA BRADLEY

Resilience comes from being focused on the poten-
tial and possibilities that exist, not the obstacles.
When I was confronted with the most diffi-
cult challenges, I instinctively looked for a foot-
hold and a way up and there would always
be someone who served as a mentor, a coach,
and a supporter who empowered me to rise.

It may be surprising to some that I am sharing my life's journey when I am just twenty-four years old and the major part of my life is still ahead of me. But I feel it is important for me to share the valuable lessons I have learned from my experiences that continue to empower me. Looking back, I realize that some of the worst times in my life carried the biggest messages or brought the greatest opportunities.

I am a certified pilot and flight instructor. I graduated with a degree in aeronautics from Embrey-Riddle Aeronautical University in Prescott, Arizona, where I was clearly different from my fellow students. I was a young black woman in a student body that was pre-dominantly white and male. I was the first in my family to graduate from high school and the first to attend college, and I am confident none of the other students spent their formative years growing up on the streets or in shelters and extended-stay budget motels.

My father lived in Denver, as did my mother and two brothers. But he was not present for us, and I grieved at his absence. I also grieved because of the emotional and psychological absence of my mother, who had her own mental, emotional, and behavioral problems and could not be there when I needed her.

I did the best I could in elementary school and did pretty well. I always made the honor roll and was placed in some gifted classes, but at one point I was denied access to classes because I had to be enrolled by a parent or caregiver. My mom had left town, so I didn't have a parent to do that. I couldn't do some school projects in elementary or middle school because there was no money for supplies, and there were times we were just sleeping on the floor of a building, or in a place without heat during Colorado's bitterly cold winters. The place where we lived was outside the school bus district, so I took public transportation to school, and that was sometimes a scary experience when people on the bus were drinking and arguing or fighting.

My older brother told me about an organization called Colorado Uplift that provides support for high school students who are in need and provides teacher/mentors and training in leadership skills. I developed a relationship with the organization, and I eventually joined its program when I was in high school. My teacher/mentor was always there to offer support and guidance, and, at one point, when my brother and I were left alone for about a week, the mentors helped to supply food and other things we needed. My mother was in mental decline, but even during that very depressing time, I always had hope that things could be better. But within a month, we ended up homeless—our landlord didn't want to renew our lease because my mother's boyfriends had damaged the place where we were living. That was the saddest time. I was the only one looking for a place where we could live with our housing voucher. But when I found a place, they wouldn't show it to me because I didn't have a driver's license and I wasn't eighteen years old.

But the horrible, traumatic parts of my life were juxtaposed with amazing and uplifting parts of my life. At the same time I was home-less and didn't even have a place to stay, I was a junior in high school, the year when we were trying to figure out what we wanted to do in life and what colleges we wanted to apply to. At this time, I was going through a lot with my mom, and it was a struggle to stay focused in school, when I was sleeping on the floor during the frigid Colorado winter. I determined I would do whatever I could to get out of that situation. In spite of it I was working, studying hard and focused on my GPA and I was involved with a number of leadership programs, leading me to scholarships and unexpected opportunities.

In my Junior year I participated in a program offered by Colorado Uplift, in which high school students learned leadership skills that we, in turn, taught to kids in elementary school and high school. At the end of the program, we were rewarded with a surprise helicopter trip above Denver. The tour was provided by a Colorado Uplift affili-ate, Prayer One, that incorporated the experience in the sky as part of its ministry.

That helicopter ride introduced me to a new perspective on both Denver and my life, sparking a vision of what I could do. Until that point, my experience of Denver was only of decrepit inner-city areas. I didn't know anything about the things that most people associate with the city: nature and the hiking and skiing. For the first time I saw the mountains and the horizon of the city and I was awestruck with how beautiful everything looked from the air. I thought that if I could always see from that perspective, I could do anything. I wanted to see myself through that lens all the time. My problems on the ground seemed so small. From that moment on, I wanted to fly and determined I would become a pilot, though I didn't know how, where, or what the task involved.

Later, Mayor Michael Hancock was the guest speaker at an event put on by another Colorado Uplift program. His presentation included a message that I needed at the time and that remains with me today. He related a parable about a man who asked for the secret to success, and he said, "When you want success as much as you need to breathe—only then will you be successful."

This spoke directly to me. I felt my head was underwater and the only way I could survive was to escape. I couldn't continue to stay underneath. I had seen where I needed to be, and I really needed that message.

Challenges and obstacles continued to emerge. There was no stability in my life and, by the time I was in the ninth grade, I had gone to eleven different schools. At one time my mother took my younger brother and moved out of the state. With nowhere to stay, I moved in with my cousin and her family. Though it still was emotionally and mentally hard for me—I was taking a daily hour and a half bus ride to and from school and sleeping with the kids in their bedroom—my cousin and her husband provided a more stable, structured environment and provided stability that I had never known.

At the time of that life-changing helicopter ride, I talked with the pilot about my dream of becoming a pilot. This was at a time when I should have been thinking about the college I wanted to go to and sending in my college and scholarship applications. I knew what I wanted to go to college for, but I didn't know what to do and how it worked.

One of the Colorado Uplift teacher/mentors told me about the Mile High Flight Program whose pilots included the local chapter of the Tuskegee Airmen. In addition to its focus on aviation, aerospace, and STEM subjects, the program strives to help its students recognize that through hard work and a good "flight plan" nothing is beyond their reach. The timing of learning about this program was amazing. The orientation to the program would be the following week. A teacher/mentor from Colorado Uplift took me and his daughter to it, and they showed us what the program would entail and how it worked. They also said that at the conclusion of the program, a scholarship would be awarded to its top student. Throughout the summer we would meet at various aviation facilities, and they would try to get us up four or five times a week, with about three hours of one-on-one instruction. It was an intensive eight-week program—on the ground, in the air, and with a lot of studying in between. And it included the opportunity for the students to make their first solo flight. That is a very big accomplishment and is the first introduction to flying and becoming a pilot.

My first solo flight was in August 2016. That was definitely frightening but also really fun and it felt so good. I had so many people supporting me. The Mile High Tuskegee pilots supported me as well as my cousin and her family, and my Colorado Uplift teacher/mentor, Miss Marcie, who has always been my rock. Later, in my work as a flight instructor, I taught for two summers and prepared students for their first solo flights.

I desperately wanted to receive that scholarship. I knew perfect attendance and submitting all my homework on time gave me a greater chance of receiving it. There were times the teacher-mentor and his daughter couldn't make it, but I took a bus, and one time a cab, to make it to the session and managed to have perfect attendance.

I ended up getting that scholarship and several others and enrolled at Embry-Riddle Aeronautical University. I met challenges throughout my university experience, and they were not always academic. Some people assumed I was there only because I was a black woman and through affirmative-action programs. But all my scholarships were based on my income level and GPA.

Still, I had to guard against self-doubt and being affected by an "imposter syndrome." Assuming that my accomplishments were due to serving as a check mark in some diversity box ignores my intelligence, determination, and hard work. But I was also reluctant to tell the story of the hurdles I'd overcome, because I never wanted to be seen as a victim or a wounded-winged bird to be pitied. I wanted to distinguish myself from my story. Throughout college I enjoyed many friendships and continued to accomplish because of all I invested in my studies.

I got my first pilot's license before starting college. To qualify to fly for an airline you must have five or six licenses. Throughout college, I worked on getting two more and, after college, I added another two, finally qualifying for an airline license. I became a commercial pilot in 2020 and joined the ranks of only a hundred and fifty black women among one hundred thousand commercial pilots. I currently work with Sky West Airline, which flies smaller planes, but contracts for flights with United, Delta, American, and Alaska. I envision the future may hold serving in corporate aviation, flying private jet aircraft, and eventually working for a large airline, but unexpected opportunities may also emerge.

Resilience comes from being focused on the potential and possibilities that exist, not the obstacles. There is so much success that people won't see, and never will see. You have to be comfortable with that and realize that people do not always have to see how much you do and how hard you had to work. They don't necessarily know all of your story, but you should continue on and do the best you can.

And when I was confronted with the most difficult challenges, I instinctively looked for a foothold and a way up and there would always be someone who served as a mentor, a coach, and a supporter who empowered me to rise.

I would tell those who are meeting challenges or obstacles in pursuing their goals that it will take a lot of work, but in the end, it is so much worth it. It's actually less work than the constant daily struggle of staying where you are. Your journey is your own, and you have the power to change anything in your life. That may mean staying on one track or deciding to change the goal you initially set for yourself. You are the only one who has the power to really affect anything in your life. Don't be stuck in a mindset because that's the easy way out or that's the way it's always been or that's the only thing you think you can achieve. You have to be able to make some hard decisions on your own to be able to change your life and those might go beyond your comfort level.

Pursue your dreams. You are the agent of your own destiny.

6

WHY QUITTING IS NOT AN OPTION

BY JON PONDER, HOPE FOR PRISONERS

No human being really wants to quit, because placed deep within the human spirit is resilience—the determination to spring back after a setback. Unfortunately, sometimes obstacles appear insurmountable.

Laptop bag and keys in hand, I headed toward my office door to turn my back on HOPE For Prisoners forever. HFP had financially hit the end of the road. My mind was on what to tell my wife and others who supported the vision that God had given me: to help formerly incarcerated men and women re-integrate into their families and the workforce. However, I never walked through the door. Instead, I learned a life-changing lesson.

During the dry seasons—when our wheels are spinning, goals are not actualized, and money is lacking—quitting becomes a tempting option. If progress is absent, questioning whether we are in the right job, the right college major or even the right relationship is normal for all of us. In the times when we face a wall that seems too tall to climb over and too wide to get around, we have two choices: retreat or rely on a stronger Source. The reason I did not follow through on my decision to quit building this organization, despite the strong urge, was because God showed me the "why" of this vision. In a split-second, I determined I would never quit, and the purpose-driven mind set that God gave me in prison was rekindled.

That first year in the federal penitentiary in Pennsylvania, several men who will never see the light of day began to mentor me. One challenged me to consider what I was going to do when I left prison. He demanded, "What do you want to do with your life?" At this juncture, I began to review my past choices and contemplate my future. More importantly, my heart was ready to dive deep into God so I could answer this question, which dealt with the concepts of meaning, purpose, and vision.

This same inmate also told me, "If a man studied one subject for one hour every day over the course of five years, he would become an expert in that subject." He looked at me and said, "What do you want to become an expert in?" His words sparked something within my heart and quickly transformed my life.

I began to acknowledge that life had meaning and could be used for good. Once I believed that not just life, but *my* life, had meaning, I could figure out my purpose and the vision required to fulfill my purpose. Interacting with these guys who were never going home, but had chosen to mentor me, was a significant demonstration of the relationship between resilience and purpose. This disposition baffled me! How do you stay fully engaged in life—model resiliency—when you do not have a release date? These men would die behind bars, but despite that, they dedicated themselves to purpose—impacting the world by investing in inmates who would reenter the world. In their hearts and minds, these men were free; the cell bars did not matter.

Webster's Dictionary defines resilience as "the capacity to withstand or recover quickly from difficulties, the ability of a substance or object to spring back into shape." When we fall, we must get up, dust ourselves off, and get back into the race that we are here to run. Resiliency causes someone to ask three questions when they are faced with a challenge:

- *How am I going to respond to this?*
- *Am I going to allow this to define who I am?*
- *How can I use this situation to move in the direction that I really want to go in life?*

I left prison in 2009 and immediately started putting the vision for HOPE For Prisoners together, launching the organization with literally five dollars to my name. This period became one of the most challenging times of my entire life. As I tried to pursue partnerships, doors were slammed in my face. People would not sit down and have a conversation with me. Why? My past reputation and my prison sentence were the obstacles. People knew I was a formerly incarcerated person who had served time, been strung out on drugs, and had participated in gang life.

In this difficult time, I was ripe to learn some powerful lessons. One was that the vastness of an obstacle tempts every human being to doubt at some point. *Is this what God has really called me to do? Was this some kind of pipe dream that I wanted?* No human being really wants to quit, because placed deep within the human spirit is resilience—the determination to spring back after a setback. Unfortunately, sometimes obstacles appear insurmountable.

I continued to step out in faith: doing this thing that God had called me to do despite the challenges. Finally, a lucrative funding opportunity came along. We had been waiting for this break, and the individual was going to contact me on a Monday with details. Monday came and went. Tuesday came and went. On Wednesday, I told the volunteers not to come back the next day, because we had reached the end of the rope. We were done. On Friday, I was by myself in my office staring at my computer. All of a sudden, an email appeared in my inbox from the individual letting me know that the deal was off. Depleted and disillusioned, I shut off my laptop. As I imagined the upcoming conversations with my wife, my pastor, and a few others, I grabbed my laptop bag and walked toward my office door to shut the light off and leave forever.

"Sit down on the couch." Talk about an abrupt halt! The voice of God put me at attention. "Sit down on the couch." I sat down on my office couch, and I heard Him say, "Do you remember when?" Then a memory came to mind—the very first visit that I had inside the detention center after my release from prison.

> *The four of us: me, the chaplain and two of the program officers walked into the elevator. As an inmate, I had been in this elevator hundreds of times. Back then, I had to walk straight in and put my face on the wall because turning your head to look around was not allowed. On this day, as I walked into the elevator with the chaplain and the others talking to me, I was caught up in a type of reverie, amazed at the contrast from my prior times in the elevator. In that overwhelming moment, I heard God say to me, "Do you see how I turned you around?"*

> *The elevator stopped and we stepped into an area in the jail where a corrections officer could see into the different units. As I stood looking into my former world from the outside, I heard God say, "Do you see what I set you free from?" Then I heard Him say, "Those people that are inside there are like my prodigal sons that have run away from me. I want them back." Then He said that there are some men that are*

*inside that don't even know who He is. God said to
me, "I love them too."*

While sitting on my office couch, reflecting on this memory, the Lord said to me, "Jon Ponder, I chose you." I was never tempted to quit HOPE For Prisoners again—I can't.

Often the temptation to quit is due to a perspective issue. When we view a mission from our limited vantage point, we will fail to comprehend the significance of that mission to God. Once the eternal value of the mission and why God chose us for the mission is considered, the temptations to quit dissolve. In my case, God knew that He needed to help me see the purpose of HOPE for Prisoners through His eyes.

Another lesson that God emphasized to me in those early years was the need for mentors. Even in my current position as Chief Executive Officer, I rely on my board members, my pastor, and other close friends to mentor me. I do absolutely nothing without going through my go-to men. Mentors become reference points, people who demonstrate what it looks like to get up after a fall or persist despite hard circumstances. Their mistakes and shortcomings, agency and determination, can be observed and humbly taken to heart. The best mentors that work in our programs are former inmates and former addicts that attended substance abuse programs. They relate to our clients' re-entry stress like no one else can.

From every direction, our clients—formerly incarcerated individuals—hear that they need to become productive members of the community. However, most have never seen positive productivity modeled, and many have never worked a legitimate job in their lives. Telling men to go home and take their rightful positions as fathers and Godly husbands is unfair, because they have not had any healthy reference point to refer to. Many of our case managers spent time in prison. Having lived that experience, they become reference points of resilience for these men and women.

The ability to relate to someone's experience serves as a catalyst for resiliency that cannot be overemphasized. One of the greatest lessons is observing how people overcome their weaknesses—how they stir themselves to stay in the fight. When I came home from prison, my oldest child, Tiffany, was addicted to heroin. Since I had struggled with drug addiction before going to prison, I felt like it was a generational curse that I passed down to her and this reality broke my heart. As a father, I tried to do everything I could to help her, but she refused my help. Finally, I realized that my only option was to let her go through what I went through. I got clean in prison, which is not an easy thing to do, because there are more drugs inside the prison system than on the streets. I went to God and laid my addiction down at the foot of the Cross. I prayed to Jesus to free me, because I could not free myself. After I completely surrendered this addiction, I walked away from drugs. My efforts to be Mr. Fix-it for my daughter and her refusals to receive my help necessitated one solution: I carried the situation to the foot of the Cross and said, "Jesus here, take this, you know this is my baby. I can't do anything for her," and I turned my back and walked away from her. Tough love. Two years later, when she asked for help, I jumped at the opportunity, but she slipped up again and wound up going to prison. After her release, she had some kids, slipped up again and went back to prison, losing custody of her kids in the process. But Tiffany is my comeback kid. Today she is clean and sober and has custody of her kids. Because of her lived experiences, I brought her on to my staff as a case manager.

Another one of our staff members, Yesenia Lopez, came into our organization about ten years ago. Her experience helps many young women realize they can overcome the most atrocious of backgrounds. When I was introduced to her, she weighed 105 pounds, was strung out on crack, and was a prostitute on the streets of Las Vegas. One of her family members had asked if we could help. As a little girl, she had been abused by her father and then turned to drugs, which is how she ended up on the streets. We sent her to a detox and substance abuse program. Afterward, she got a job and stayed engaged with HFP. We helped her go back to school and she became a substance abuse counselor. At that point, I brought her on my staff. However, her overcoming did not stop there. She earned a master's degree, became a licensed Certified Alcohol and Drug Counselor (CADC), and owns her own counseling center. Her life could have deteriorated—this happens to so many—but her example of resilience demonstrates that given the correct support, any person can come up and out of those situations. After she overcame her personal challenges, she turned right around to help other people.

Bob Woodson says all the time, "we need to study that"—meaning that we need to understand every factor that helps people like this not only overcome, but also turn around and extend a hand. Not everyone comes up out of those situations and prospers. So, yes, we need to study that!

Men and women who pursue their purpose must accept that not everyone is going to cheer them onward, and for this reason, they must learn to live with the challenges of opposition. Resiliency will help them hear the critics and keep on trekking. When the world tells them "No," they must hold onto the moment when they received their commission and heard a "Yes."

This "yes" raises people above the tide of doubt that will occur at times, especially when a vision seems bigger than their level of education or takes them outside their comfort zone. The "yes" sloughs off feelings of inadequacy. The temptation to compare and compete with others must be resisted because not only does it discredit a person's unique gifts and skillset, but it also wastes energy that needs to be funneled into the vision. Men and women must have faces like flint, eyes fixed forward, not roving to and fro to see what the next person is doing or hear what people are saying. No other human being's approval is necessary. Individuals must withstand the doubt, the questions, and the closed doors, and keep pressing toward their goal. When people see a mission from His eyes, they will withstand any pressure that arises.

7

STAY THE COURSE

BY BRIAN WADE,
THE GENESIS CENTER AND THE ALPHA HOUSE

*Resilience helped me trust God when He abruptly
changed my plans. Running The Genesis Center
required me to adjust to new ways of living and
paying the bills. I had to let God work out every
detail instead of taking situations into my own hand.*

Attending nineteen schools before I graduated from high
school gave me a fighter's mentality, because in each new
school, I had to stand my ground against bullies, resist fear
to make new friends, and stay true to the principles taught to me by
my parents, who were church planters. Constant change helped me
understand that God, not other people or temporal circumstances,
is my source of security. My boyhood experience also taught me to
expect challenges and stay the course.

Looking back, I see that God was shaping me into a person who
could withstand the rejection and criticism that comes with a calling that contradicts the status quo. Me, a white pastor living with
his wife and kids among non-white addicts to help them find freedom. The Genesis Center and our sister ministry The Alpha House
serve addicts—people who are largely transient, who because of their

lifestyle do not usually get the follow-up or sustained support needed to end their addiction.

Our first step to opening the rescue mission was to put an advertisement in the local newspaper. It said: "Wanted: drug addicts, drug dealers, gang bangers, homosexuals, prostitutes…by Jesus Christ." Based on that one and only advertisement, the word spread, and we received people from everywhere. We stay conscious of attitudes and lifestyles of addicts, help them navigate the withdrawal process, introduce them to Jesus, and give them a place to live where they can have a safe community as long as they need.

Every difficulty is an opportunity. Local government departments, pastors, and residents were slow to endorse this work that God called me into, but my disposition helped me stay the course and focus on God and the addicts, not the squabbles and the skepticism. Now having done this work for two decades, I am convinced that God will use every experience in our pasts to prepare us for our mission in life. Nothing is wasted, and by helping me activate resilience and face each challenge, God has demonstrated this beautifully.

Our adventure began when God asked us to leave our comfortable lifestyle and start a rescue mission for people with addictions. When God sets people on a mission, not only will He work out the logistics, but he also uses the process to teach people lessons. The theme for many of my lessons was giving up self-reliance. How does self-reliance tie into resilience? For me, giving up my ways of doing things meant surrendering to God's ways of doing things and for any human mindset, that feels risky. But resilience motivated me to trust God when He abruptly changed my plans. Running The Genesis Center required me to adjust to new ways of living and paying the bills. I had to let God to work out every detail instead of taking situations into my own hand.

1999: The closing date on our new house was three days away, and we were excited. Our new home reflected the success that I had experienced in the business I owned. As I was sitting in my office, I sensed God saying that we were not supposed to buy this house. I had a solid relationship with the Lord, so I had no problem letting Him know the displeasure and confusion that I felt at that moment. After a few minutes of back-and-forth conversation, God to human son, I said, "I refuse to tell my wife. If this is You, You are going to have to tell her." An hour or so later, my wife came into my office with a strange look on her face and said, "I get the impression that we are not supposed to go through with the closing."

At the time, I was bi-vocational—running a business and doing ministry—and I tried not to figure out what God was doing and why, but only trust Him. I had to bear with the weird looks and silent criticisms of others, but to stay the course of my conviction. I knew we had heard from God. Our realtor respected our decision but reminded us that we would lose our $10,000 deposit. However, because I believed in His goodness, losing the $10,000 deposit for canceling the contract was not something I believed He would have us do. I told the realtor that.

Understandably, the sellers were upset—they had scheduled a big yard sale to get rid of extra furniture and other items. Ironically, a couple attending the yard sale asked the sellers if they could see what they had missed. The wife told this couple that the house was being relisted the following day and then allowed them to walk through it. At the end of the tour, the couple offered to pay cash, and because they were able to close quickly, we got our deposit back.

In this situation, I had to mentally stay the course of trusting in the heart of God. I could not begin to worry about where we were going to go, since our current house had already been sold. I refused to let myself plan how I was going to get the money to pay a penalty. So, resilience requires mental toughness.

We moved out of our home to embrace days and nights housed in an old church building we rented to use as the residence for alcoholics and drug addicts. Because we no longer had a home mortgage, we reasoned that my business would cover all the expenses. I thought we'd live among the residents for about six months and told my wife this. It ended up being seven years.

The next major faith challenge came the day when God impressed upon my heart to sell my business and commit full-time to the rescue mission. Since I was bi-vocational, working a hundred hours per week was not uncommon, and once again, I neither liked nor agreed with His request. I prayed and wrestled with God for weeks about this, wondering how the bills would get paid. His answer was, "Brian I don't want to be dependent upon you, I want you to be dependent upon me." So, I gave my business away.

For the first six months working full-time for the mission, I did what I had always done: sales. For years I had done financial planning, specifically estate succession for people of wealth, and using these skills, I decided to meet with pastors and business leaders to market the ministry and ask them to support us. On my mind were the bills that needed to be paid.

One day when I was in prayer the Lord challenged me to review why I was using my skill as a salesman to grow the ministry. "Brian, show me one dime that you have brought in as a result of your efforts." I couldn't. Although I had been meeting with many people, I had no results. Then He said, "Brian, I want you to take your signature off of my ministry." Instantly, I knew what He meant: I was building the ministry according to my reasoning and my strategy, instead of seeking Him for guidance at every step.

This mission required us to rely less on our prior ministry experience and vocational knowledge, and more on His step-by-step guidance. Faith-building testimonies were part of my heritage, but because God wanted to be sole supplier of our needs, my wife and I had to come into a different place of faith.

God always proved His faithfulness as I abandoned the temptation to take issues into my own hands. For example, one time we did not have the money to pay the gas bill. I called every addict and staff member into the sanctuary. Together, as co-residents, we put the gas bill on the altar. We prayed and soon the money came in. That was not an isolated event. We have lived in total reliance on God ever since God told me to cancel the contract, sell my business, and go full-time. No hardship, no challenge was wasted; God used every challenge to build our confidence in Him.

We lived with the addicts and shared meals together. We've seen incredible miracles and transformations in people's lives. We have seen people come to Christ, and we have been able to redistribute material resources that were donated to us. Everything we have is because God gave it. This ministry has His signature. No longer am I designing what it will become.

Resilience must be demonstrated. There's an old saying: "we've done so much with so little for so long, we now believe we can do anything with nothing." My kids live like that. My daughter is now twenty-five, but when she was young, she wanted a pair of Barbie rollerblades. I remember hearing her pray for them because I could not afford to buy them. Within a week, two pairs of rollerblades showed up in donations for the ministry. My daughter asked and God delivered. My children's confidence in Him grew way beyond our human ability to teach them, because I let go and let God be who He says He is. Staying the course despite the challenges we faced was worth it to impart faith to another generation.

Getting a word from God has the power to empower us through obstacles. Very early on, I did not know what God was doing. A point came when the city told us that we could not use the church for a mission because of the zoning. The problem was we already had people living there. I did not have much money, so a Board member volunteered to go downtown, fill out the paperwork and pay the $100 fee.

The city told him that we could not rezone it for our use, and they sent a cease-and-desist order with twenty-four hours to vacate the premises. My Board member got to my office in tears, saying "They are going to shut us down." But I had a word from God. I had done exactly what God told me to do, exactly the way He told me to do it. So, I knew this was not the end and I told this to my Board member. This battle with the city lasted about a year, but we never moved. My confidence was strong despite this obstacle, because I had a word from God.

In this journey, being resilient was based on being anchored in God—knowing that He would do what He said He would do. Surrendering to His perfect destiny for me, in those moments where I did not like what He was doing, caused me to tap into a level of resilience that I would not have experienced otherwise. I knew sales; I did not know about addiction. I knew my white Christian culture; I did not know the ways of other ethnicities. I knew how to rely on myself, my skills and know-how, but I needed to develop a greater ability to rely completely on God. This lesson of surrender helped me to help the wonderful men and women in our programs, as well as my children, learn how to rely completely on God.

Moses went through a similar journey of abandoning self-reliance and staying resilient in the faith of his fathers. Growing up in the palace of Egypt was not a wasted experience. God used his upbringing to teach him lessons for leadership. I never imagined myself doing a rescue mission for addicts. Everything I do, I had to learn. Everything we have, He provided. At one time, I heard Him say, "When I am finished with this, it will have to be said that no man has done this."

When our relationship with God becomes the root of our life, although we will sometimes feel inadequate or unprepared, we can surrender to the right-turns that He tells us to make. Despite these unexpected shifts, we have to realize that the preparation for the shift had started long before, often beginning in childhood. Although the

Lord told me to set aside my plans and skills, He used my capacity to adapt, which came because of all the schools I attended. Although I had to get my family used to an entirely different lifestyle, He used our deep heritage of faith to help us stay the course and prevail.

8

TORI HOPE PETERSEN; FROM FOSTER CHILD TO MRS. UNIVERSE

BY CHARLES LOVE

Tori's case exemplifies resilience. She overcame difficult odds and was forced to endure situations that must have seemed impossible to overcome at the time. She developed the traits necessary to cope and made a conscious decision not to be a victim.

Resilience is the ability to cope with and recover from setbacks. It is seen as toughness, a trait that greatly increases the likelihood of overcoming obstacles. While some people have an easier time being resilient than others, it is a skill that can be honed. Unfortunately, many believe it is a natural ability—something you are either born with or you lack. They view resilient people as superheroes.

In reality, resilient people have many of the same fears and doubts that others do. Somehow, they find a way to fight through them and become successful despite the fears and doubts not due to an absence of them. It also is important to note that no matter how determined one is to get beyond setbacks and trauma, those who overcome adversity will always need help along the way. This is the case with Tori Hope Petersen.

Tori entered the world through strife. Her mom, a victim of human trafficking at fourteen, was arrested for solicitation of prostitution. While in custody, she went into labor in the back of a police car and gave birth to Tori while handcuffed to a hospital bed.

What should have been a happy moment for her was filled with anxiety. When she found out she was pregnant, she also tested positive for HIV, but was hopeful her new baby would not suffer the same fate. When the doctor told her that the baby was fine and her test was a false positive, she saw it as a sign of victory and hope, and her daughter was aptly named Victoria Hope.

Tori's first stint with the foster care system came when she was just three years old. Her mother and Jack, the man Tori knew as her father, were sleeping when the police burst through the door and started searching their home. They were arrested, and Tori was placed in a foster home. This would not be her last venture into the foster care system.

Surprisingly, her first example of resiliency came from her mom. Throughout her troubled past and struggles with mental illness, she tried her best for Tori. She got married and got a respectable job. Tori saw her mom portray a strong work ethic, lead others, and become successful at something. She also encouraged Tori to go to college.

By the time Tori was nine years old, however, her mom had experienced several mental breakdowns and a suicide attempt for which she was hospitalized. Unfortunately, her marriage failed shortly after becoming pregnant with Tori's sister. This is when her mother started verbally and physically abusing Tori, often calling her a product of rape and telling her she was, "a spitting image of a rapist."

Looking for a father figure, Tori began regularly spending the night at her Uncle Allen's house. One night, he crawled into bed with her. After this, she tried to limit her interactions with him. It was complicated. He had saved her from many of her mother's "manic" episodes. Living between two abusers was emotionally draining, so she finally told her mom about the abuse—only to have her mother tell her that he had done the same thing to her.

When she was in seventh grade, a teacher noticed the bruises on her body, and she was temporarily placed with her mother's cousins. After getting into a fight with one of their children, the caseworker called her mother to come pick her up, even though there was a court order preventing her from seeing Tori. This was not the only time this happened.

Common sense says that knowingly placing a child back in an abusive environment should never happen, but Tori never blamed the caseworkers. She understood the caseworkers had unmanageable caseloads and were often put in impossible positions. They are often short of homes for children to go to, so when they must leave a foster home, they have few options. Tori's mom was the only person they could call.

This can also occur when there is an accusation of abuse or neglect in a foster home. Often there are several foster children in the home, and if there is a report about one child, all of the children have to be removed. The social workers simply have nowhere to place them. So sometimes, they weigh the risks and overlook the abuse. This is what happened with Tori's sister.

The beatings Tori received from her mother escalated. After one such occurrence, Tori hit her mom back and was arrested. At the hearing scheduled to determine how Tori would be charged, her mom verbally berated her and her GAL (guardian ad litem). Because of the outburst, the judge ruled that her mom was too mentally unstable to have custody of her kids. Tori and her sister were placed in foster care.

They were fortunate enough to be placed in a foster home together, but shortly after arriving there, Tori's sister told her that the foster parent's biological son sexually abused her. Tori called the caseworker to report the abuse, but when the foster parent accused her of lying, she was sent to a group home and her sister was forced to stay in the house with her abuser. Tori was thirteen years old and her sister was only four years old. Yet again, the system failed her.

The group home was worse than a foster home. A cold facility with several girls sharing sleeping quarters, the home was designed for children with mental or behavioral problems. There was strict oversight managed by a point system; Tori felt she didn't belong there. However, there was one positive aspect of the visit: mandated group counseling. She had been going to church since arriving at the group home and credits this along with the counseling for helping to change her perspective. Despite all that had happened, she forgave her mother and started to heal.

She told herself, "While I didn't have to take responsibility for the trauma caused to me, I did need to take responsibility for my own healing and decide what I would do about it." She started her growth by affirming that she was not a victim. The things that happened to her would not define her. She was also starting to develop a level of self-worth.

After nearly a year at the group home Tori was placed in another foster home. She was finally at the point where she would accept help, and God began sending her the encouragement she needed.

First, there was her eighth-grade English teacher. Because of the mental stress and abrupt changes in living conditions, Tori was struggling in school. Mr. Rodenberger encouraged her to focus on her grades. He told her this was the point where her grades would be on her permanent record, and she could make the necessary changes now. She went from getting Cs and Ds to As and Bs.

In high school, Tori took an interest in painting and got permission to paint a mural outside her English teacher's class. Mr. Clark would spend his lunch hour with her and discuss religion as she painted. He never pushed her, but he showed her she had value and purpose, strengthening her resiliency and challenging her perception of Christians.

Next there was Gigi. After several additional foster homes and another stint in a group home, Tori was placed with her. She was kind, sincere, and did not try too hard to be either a disciplinarian or a friend. She supervised Tori's track practices and took her to her post-secondary classes. More importantly, Gigi helped her find her faith. Tori wanted to believe but had met too many "Christians" that did not truly live as she thought Christians should. Gigi completed the change in perception of Christians that Mr. Clark had started.

Tori's strongest advocate and mentor was her track coach, Scott Wichman. He supported her, encouraged her, and loved her. He told her if she worked hard, she could win the state track championship. He also told her that he would like her to be part of his family. But that could not happen until the season was over. She was about to turn eighteen and had a big decision to make.

Tori decided that when she turned eighteen, she wanted to emancipate herself out of the foster care system. Many assume you age out of the system, but there is extended foster care for those with no place to go. Tori wanted none of it; she wanted her freedom. She was reminded by teachers, caseworkers, lawyers, and community members about the saddening statistics of foster care. Foster kids are more likely to experience behavioral, mental and physical health issues; homelessness, employment and academic difficulties; drug abuse; early parenthood; incarceration, and other potentially lifelong adversities. She knew the statistics, but Tori was determined to prove them wrong.

When the judge ruled in her favor, Tori was elated. Although she cried happy tears, she still had no idea where she would go. She could not stay with Gigi, who would have lost her foster care license, and she could not stay with Scott, since the season had not ended. Her mom asked her to live with her, but she knew that was the last place she should go. So, she relied on the kindness of others, sleeping for days or weeks at a time wherever she could. But she was free.

Tori would go on to win four championship titles in one meet, and after the season ended, she went to live with Scott's family permanently. She was so grateful that she changed her last name to Wichman. Years later, when she married, Scott walked her down the aisle.

Tori's case exemplifies resilience. She overcame difficult odds and was forced to endure situations that must have seemed impossible to overcome at the time. She developed the traits necessary to cope and made a conscious decision not to be a victim. Tori's story also highlights the importance of having help along the way.

At key moments in her life, Tori found people who supported her. From the teacher who helped her focus on her studies, to the high school teacher who spent his lunch hour talking to her about religion, from the people who helped usher her to her faith in God, to Scott who mentored her, loved her, and helped her win a state title—people lifted her up when she needed it, sometimes even encouraging her to take on new challenges.

By the time she was twenty-five, Tori was married with two biological kids and three foster children. With the demands of five children under five, she didn't have time for much else. So, when a friend suggested she enter a beauty pageant, she laughed. However, when she considered her days of sweatpants and crying children, she jumped at the idea of a chance to "get pretty." With the continued support of her family and friends, she won the 2021 Mrs. Universe International title.

None of this diminishes her resilience. In fact, it is a credit to her that she accepted their help. Because of her history of abuse and neglect, and the disregard she experienced living in a dozen foster homes, it would have been easy to reject offers of assistance—assuming they were not sincere or came with strings attached. Accepting help is an important part of resiliency.

Tori is an inspiration to anyone dealing with trauma. She is a college graduate, a former track and field all-American, a former Mrs. Universe, and a best-selling author. She wrote her book, *Fostered: One Woman's Powerful Story of Finding Faith and Family through Foster Care*, to help struggling children know they are not victims and there is a way out.

Tori is currently a public speaker and foster care advocate. She is the founder of Beloved Initiative, a non-profit serving vulnerable communities and individuals who have experienced abuse. She also helped Hillsdale College start Fostering the Good, a fund setup to help ease the financial burden for kids in the foster care system. She is also a wife, mother of two biological kids and an adopted young adult son, and she rescued her younger sister from foster care.

She believes, "We have power to transform trauma, to minimize it, deepen it, or be a part of its healing. Where trauma comes through vessels that are cruel and cold, we can be vessels of mercy and warmth."

9

ENLARGING MY HUMANITY: HOW TEACHING KU KLUX KLAN COLLEGE STUDENTS GAVE ME RESILIENCE AND A PATH BACK TO GOD

BY JASON D. HILL, PH.D.

Resilience is a blessing that has to be cultivated.
There were mornings when I hated attending
classes, and there were Saturday mornings when
I drove to the tutorials with horrific stomach
cramps, a palpitating heart and sweating palms.

My first teaching job, after earning my doctorate in philosophy in the fall of 1998, was assistant professor of philosophy at Southern Illinois University in Edwardsville (SIUE). I had been awarded my Ph.D. from Purdue University the previous spring. My teaching schedule for the academic year—fall and the next spring semester—was two courses in moral philosophy and critical thinking/logic. I had declined a more lucrative offer from Bentley College in Waltham, Massachusetts because the teaching load was lighter at SIUE, and I had big plans to overhaul my dissertation, rewrite it, and add new chapters. I planned to turn it into a compelling book, and I subsequently did. Of the five books that I have authored, that first book retains a special place in my heart. It remains in print twenty-three years after publication.

I faced my logic class as a recovering atheist, someone for whom atheism was no longer an option. However, I could not quite bring my will to yield to my desires—I was a praying agnostic. I should have been elated. I was in a great relationship, I was a newly minted Ph.D., and I was teaching in a school of my choice. Yet my heart was heavy. There was a void; an emptiness that I could not explain lingered in the pit of my stomach. I felt impatient, a bit irritable at times, and hungry for greater meaning and purpose in life than the ones I had created for myself.

Most of my students were white, poor and undereducated. Many of them lived in trailer parks, some without running water. There were a handful of black students from East St. Louis who sequestered themselves on one side of the room away from the white students.

Commanding the attention of the students at the beginning of each class was challenging. They were a noisy bunch who would often talk among themselves during class—much to my consternation. Often, I would simply stop talking and let their verbal drivel run a long course. When the background noise which was my voice had faded, they would stop talking. I would look at them for a long time and then quietly return to the material at hand. Invariably, to take advantage of their loquaciousness, I'd ask them some questions about the material they were required to have read. Invariably, they had no responses.

When one of my students—we'll call him Daniel—re-handed me his exam one afternoon with a handwritten note that read, "I could choose to bring a gun to school, but I suppose I will accept the D you gave on my exam." I literally pinched my arm in my office, to remind myself of the gratitude I felt after living in the United States for (at the time) thirteen years. I felt gratitude and pride for having earned four college degrees, for becoming a university professor who had a big-name publisher interested in publishing my first book. I felt gratitude that all my dreams were coming true—and that now I would have to decide how to deal with an obstreperous kid in my class.

I dug my hands into my pocket and clenched the large gold-plated crucifix I had carried as a ritual for the past year. It was a ritual meant to initiate godhead inside me. I did not know exactly how it would work, but holding the crucifix and feeling it pressed against my leg brought me a feeling of peace and utter assuredness that, for a brief while, everything would be well.

The next evening after classes were over found me in the small town of Vandalia purchasing gas for my truck before heading for the commute to St. Louis where I lived. After our next class meeting, two white female students came to my office. They were nervous. They had something urgent to speak to me about.

Once I assured them of confidentiality, they told me the following: they advised against going to Vandalia to purchase gas, because a lot of Klan members lived there, so many that it was informally known to a lot of folks as "Klandalia." They did not think that it was safe for me, as a black person, to be there after dark. I encouraged them to continue, and they told me most of the white students in the class—about 80 percent of them, they surmised—were in the Klan, or they came from households where parents were Klan members. They looked a bit embarrassed, assuring me they were not in the Klan. They cautioned me against a student named Daniel, the student who wore a skull ring. It was a Klan ring and there was a "mark" on it, they confessed, that indicated that he "had put the hurt on somebody—probably a black person."

I'm not sure what emotions I felt that night as I lay in bed and thought of what the students had told me. I remembered the ring lying against Daniel's paper as he had handed me the exam with his threatening message. I remembered a kindly warning another black professor had issued to me the week before classes began: I was to be extra conciliatory towards the students, to treat them more as clients, and not to be punitive towards any of them no matter how they might comport themselves in classes or towards me.

I slept with the crucifix on the pillow next to me that night. I did not say much of a prayer. I did not speak with God. That which I would have asked for had already been granted. Tomorrow's unfolding would change my life in a way I could not have conceived of as yet. I somehow felt prayers would have been superfluous; tomorrow had already arrived.

I fell asleep quickly, knowing that resilience, perseverance, and tenacity were the traits I would need to get through the year. I slept deeply that night.

The next morning, I stood by the lectern and laid down the law. In a forceful but quiet voice, I told them that I would never tolerate disrespect from any of them, that I did not care who among them or their families were members of the Klan, that I had grown up in Jamaica—a very violent country—and that I had witnessed violent atrocities that would break the toughest among them in half.

This was my ship. I'd have anyone who showed even a patina of disrespect towards me permanently removed from the class.

I told them they needed to refrain from referring to themselves as dumb farm kids, as that was a sort of disrespect towards themselves that I would not tolerate. Self-deprecation of that nature had no place in my class. Unlearn your addiction to self-evisceration, I advised them. I told them they had a humanity that they had to achieve, that it was not an endowment, that life existed as a series of continued disclosures and possibilities. "You all have a not-yet-self, a self in becoming, a self on which you can pin an aspirational identity—one which ought to be suffused with a commitment to excellence, discipline, ambition, resilience and perseverance."

One student asked me why she should embody those virtues, when bad things would eventually happen to good persons like herself.

I responded by saying, "Bad things will happen to good people and bad people alike. Suffering is built into the nature of existence. You must cultivate your goodness, because it is the source from which you will heal from the bad things that will inevitably happen to you. No one ever healed from a source of evil or character rot."

I told them they could make a choice about how to interpret their lives. They could accept the narratives they had inherited from their families and culture; or they could revise and modify those narratives that informed their thinking and their identities. They could decide what they wanted to become and work towards that vision.

As I uttered those words, I peered at their faces. Some looked as if they were on the verge of tears; some looked contemptuous, as if I were uttering idealistic sophomoric verbiage that had no basis in their reality. Others appeared thoughtful, and some seemed worried. I realized, too, that a significant portion of them were failing the class. Suddenly, it seemed as if some other voice took possession of me, and I said, "I'll be holding free tutorials in my office on Saturday from 10 a.m. to 1 p.m. I know some of you work during the week, and it's often difficult to meet during my official office hours."

Some of them nodded. They all looked somber. I knew these extra tutorial sessions would bleed into the time I usually spent working on my book. Since I was also in a long-distance relationship with a professor at Cornell University, there would be weekends when I would not be available.

Three months into the tutorials, we were doing more than reviewing logic. My primary goal was to improve their skill set in the subject and have them leverage it in other disciplines. I learned about their lives and the hardships they faced. I acknowledged their resilience, tenacity and perseverance, and assured them that these were unassailable virtues.

I asked them if they had issues with receiving conceptual instructorship from a black man who was their professor, given that none of them had had a black instructor before. Some admitted that they did have such issues. Their parents had taught them that black people were stupid by nature, and that white people were superior because they were white. I didn't sound stupid, one student volunteered, so he wondered if I was an exception to the rule. I told him that I could adduce myself as evidence that what they were taught was simply wrong, but I asked them to imagine that—because they practically lived in a closed system—they were unable to meet the thousands of people such as myself who did exist in the world. Daniel, the student with the skull ring who had written the threatening letter, asked me if I disliked the students as a group. He was standing by the door of the office. He had never once entered my office. The ten other students who attended the tutorials had found ways to squeeze themselves inside my small office—some sat on the floor, others in the concave of the window. I looked at him for a while, then told him that dislike for students whose education I was responsible for was not an emotion conducive to learning. His dismissive smirk prompted me to say, "I dislike the idea of what you, Daniel, will permanently grow into if you choose to remain rooted to a belief system that posits the existence of other people as problems, simply because they have immutable characteristics different than yours."

He looked incredulous. "You asked for it by asking me what I thought," I said.

At nights I often descended into loneliness. A void anchored itself in my chest. I prayed fervently at times. The tutorials were definitely having a marked improvement on the performance of those who chose to attend, although, sadly, not one of my black students from St. Louis were among them. When I gently reminded them after class about the tutorials on Saturday mornings, most smiled politely.

Others said: "We're good, professor."

I wondered what I was hoping to truly achieve in these tutorials with a pack of racists. What was my ultimate goal? I sat on my couch one evening after classes and realized I had asked God for a sign and that he had given it to me. In serving those students I was not developing a calcified heart or becoming regretful that I had accepted a job with such stark challenges.

In those tutorials, I had stripped away every protective artifice and mask—somehow. I faced the students with my naked singularity and a degree of vulnerability. Retrospectively, I realized that God was stripping me to a thin core; that such was the only way to encounter the students with moral integrity.

Behind the carapace of indifference and toughness they exhibited lay ugly wounds and a great deal of hurt and suffering. I was not there to be a therapist. But in being unafraid of them, and in revealing the core of who I was, they would see there was nothing to fight or resent in me in order to protect and preserve their lives. The only thing that was left shining in that core was love; it was a universal love that—in a very abstract form—was the subject of my book. It was a love that was able to get behind and beyond the masks and ideologies they were formed by. They were second-hand consumers of values and belief systems that they had not ratified through appraisal, or by answering the question: Do these beliefs, values and mores fit the core of who I am?

One afternoon as the tutorial was ending, I asked them to ponder a question I often asked myself and others who were willing to make themselves vulnerable to the vicissitudes of life's challenges—and who wanted to find, or even approximate, their core. The question was: Who were you before the world told you who you had to be and had to become?

Resilience is a blessing that has to be cultivated. There were mornings when I hated attending classes, and there were Saturday mornings when I drove to the tutorials with horrific stomach cramps, a palpitating heart and sweating palms.

God had granted me grace. I knew that had I stepped into those tutorials in full professorial mode, or with a smug sense of superiority over what several regarded those students to be—village idiots and social ballasts—that I would have failed miserably in my task. But I felt that God was saving two birds with one firm and gentle touch. In stripping me to a thin core so I could reach the humanity of my students, God was also stripping away all the defense mechanisms and highly intellectualized mediating tropes that stood in the way of my fully approaching Him and knowing Him.

At the end of the academic year, some of the students cried when I announced that I would be leaving to assume another teaching position. Some even hugged me and wept bitterly. No one had ever spoken to them like that, one young woman told me. Daniel shook my hand and thanked me for all I had done for him. With a smile on my face, I reminded him to never refer to himself as a dumb farm kid. I wished them well in their pursuits. I encouraged them to keep in touch. I handed each of the black students from East St. Louis my professional card and told them to reach out if they just needed to be in touch. I was unsentimental in my farewell.

I realized the worst in anyone can be an accident of circumstances that have not been mediated by others who have the power to alter the trajectory of a damaged life. There were genuflective and redemptive moments in those tutorials. They came with the realization that when we parse through our beliefs and past actions, and we examine the suffering that we have inflicted on others, we constitute a confederacy of sinners who are striving for redemption and reconciliation.

Why had the parents of the students (they all lived at home) permitted them to come to a black professor's office for tutorials, if they believed in the congenital inferiority of black people?

People are often drawn to the extremes in others that they lack in themselves. Perhaps the cosmopolitan in me, the lover of humanity and the citizen of the world, had found some attraction in the philosophical antipode of those sentiments: in the atavistic tribal cravings, in those who believed in some primordial form of chemical predestination and biological collectivism as insignias of moral and metaphysical superiority. I needed to be immersed in this racist paradigm to truly understand it.

When I showed a colleague Daniel's threatening letter, I was informed by the school administration that I could be assigned another class. I refused the offer. This was my cross to carry, I thought. But why should it be my cross to carry? What justification was there for any black person who had been placed in such a precarious position to participate in and transform a hostile classroom environment?

I believe that if you're resilient in life you learn, among other things, to parent yourself—to nurture yourself and take care of your own needs. Sometimes, with the help of an active moral imagination, I looked upon those students and thought: There but for the grace of God go I! As I extended my moral imagination farther, I realized that if I did not tutor these students, I would be writing them out of the historical process—relegating them to the dustbin of history in my own mind. Misanthropy was not an option.

I believe that on those Saturday mornings as I parked my truck and walked to my office, that I was walking to minister more to the souls of those students than I was in improving their skill set in logic. The tutorials took on a religious meaning. I had asked God to give me a sign. He gave me a task instead, one that led straight to individuals ensconced in a milieu of hatred. The ideology of hate commanded them to descend into total ignorance and hatred. It appealed to the lowest common denominator within them. I had no script, for the notes and diagrams on logic were not the scripts; they were preambles to a greater mode of being in their presence. If love, among other things, is a command to rise in the name of the best within oneself, then was I placing too much of a burden on myself by offering up myself as an incentive for them to rise to the noblest and most heroic vision of themselves, that they could be taught to seek and find?

The Saturday tutorials became part of God's gifted rituals for me to draw closer to Him, while simultaneously exposing and sharing that element of the divine He imparted in me to my students.

I reasoned that if we were all made in God's image then, somehow, I had to affirm the students surrounding me. I needed to inoculate them against a poisonous world—not through proselytizing and guilt-tripping, but by means of my own agency. I did not have to become anything in particular—stripping myself to a thin core revealed a self that, in its nakedness, would be able to fulsomely reflect the divinity that resided there. If they could see it, then perhaps they would be moved to get outside themselves and their hermetically sealed history and move into a capacious future. And hopefully the picture of the good, the true, and the beautiful, that I had painted as suffusing all spheres of life, would be fuel for them in the days ahead, as hopefully they cultivated goodness within themselves. That cultivated goodness, I hoped, would save them from the inevitable suffering they would face in their lives, and from the charged infections of the soul that afflict anyone who judges another by any criterion other than the content of his or her character.

10

LAW, LIBERTY, LOVE, AND LAND

BY MICHAEL D. C. BOWEN

*This life of service and growth showed me that
the new black nation was within myself. It
wasn't a destination for escape from America. It
was an old part of America I could make new.*

"L aw, liberty, love, and land." At this moment in my life,
my own childhood memories are more vivid than my
father's, vague and absent, as he approaches eighty-
seven years of age in ill health. These words were his way of succinctly
describing his requirements for a new Black nation within or apart
from the United States. He was a black nationalist, and I was the first
of his five children of the new generation, born Negro, raised Black,
and proud.

As often as it is discussed and debated, described and deformed,
the matter of blackness has always been nothing more or less than the
human story. America in its history and confusion may have sustained
doubts about the human nature of the Negro, but this was never my
problem. Neither in recognizing the doubts of others or in harboring
doubts about myself had my human nature ever been in question. I
was the boy born to a loving family, and if other people could not

understand, then perhaps it would be clearer under a new flag. After all, we had all of human history thus far to study and do things right.

My father was born in New Haven, Connecticut. My mother was born in New Orleans, Louisiana. They met in New York City, joining two remarkably different families into something new. Both their collegiate training in sociology, and his particular discipline as a U.S. Marine, had a significant impact on my growing up. After his honorable discharge, both were caught up and contributing to their professions as they became social workers for the expanding Los Angeles County Department of Public Social Services (DPSS).

They moved to a small apartment in the West Adams neighborhood of Los Angeles, just around the corner from the headquarters of Golden State Mutual Life, the largest black-owned insurance company in America. My mother put on her best white gloves and pocketbook for her interview at a small administrative building east of LA and was hired on the spot. Dad worked at the new DPSS building on West Adams Boulevard and South Grand Avenue. Their jobs were to help poor families in need, but soon they found themselves going beyond, by organizing and networking with other job seekers, helping them pass the newly desegregated Civil Service exams.

As our own family grew, so did my parents' ambitions. Taking on the scholarly bearing of his own self-taught father, his Ph.D. brother, and his tough-minded sister, Dad began writing a series of essays and maintained correspondence with many notable individuals in the new Black Consciousness, Black Nationalist, and Black Arts movements. He established his own small Institute for Black Studies in 1966 in the wake of the Watts Riots. We became family friends with Dr. Alfred Ligon, owner of the first and largest black bookstore in California. Ligon was a philosopher and metaphysician whose kindness and noble bearing was inspired by mysticism. His Aquarian Bookstore was named after the anticipated Age of Aquarius. He also ran the Aquarian Center, which attracted a varied coterie of movement-creative individuals like the Watts Poets (my father was the eldest of the Watts Poets) and the inventor of Kwanzaa, Ron Karenga. By 1968, Dad had purchased a house and converted the two-car garage into a stage for the production of plays. This was the Redwood Theater Group, which provided a venue for aspiring artists. He published *Circle Magazine.* Ever the role-model mother for her social work and in the neighborhood, Mom ran the Children's Workshop. I helped Dad with the mimeograph machine for *Patterns,* our newsletter.

In our heyday, I studied Swahili. We talked about emigrating out of the U.S. to Brazil's new capital of Brasilia, where the socialists were giving out free parcels of land. An uncle on my mother's side was one of the first Peace Corps representatives in Francophone West Africa. My father and I were interviewed on television on the Louis Lomax show. I can remember riding in several fancy cars in Watts' Summer Festival parades. But several things diverted our trajectory, despite our memorization of every verse of James Weldon Johnson's "Black National Anthem." It was Robert Jr, born with spinal meningitis.

The retelling of our story goes many ways. Maybe it was the conviction that the FBI was tapping our phones. Maybe it was the brick that barely missed my pregnant mother's head in our last street protest against the legendary racial covenants of Torrance, CA. Maybe it was the discovery of the weapons of certain movement members. Maybe it was the personality clashes between my father and Karenga. I tend to think it was the birth of my baby brother "Scoobie," whose miracle recovery from spinal meningitis puzzled all the specialists at Kaiser Sunset (where all my sibs were born). Mom rediscovered Christianity in evangelical form as only a lapsed Catholic can do. My father discovered that fatherhood was much more important than any of his more radical dreams and rediscovered his Episcopalian roots. Most importantly, I think, is that he discovered the mountains.

By the time there were five of us kids, Dad had to sell the sporty little German cars he had collected. Gone were the ragtop Volkswagen and the Porsche 356. Now there was only the VW Bus with the sliding door and removable seat. Purchased from the dealership on Crenshaw and 30th Street, the yellowish-tannish underpowered beast carried us many times from West Adams to the wilderness of the Angeles National Forest.

We grew closer as a different kind of family as the violence of the '60s wore down everyone's willingness to clash. But there was nothing ever in my parents' minds about clashing. They were simply determined to help in every way. Soon, my father was appointed Special Assistant to the Director of the Los Angeles County Health Department. He got a shiny new white Chevy Vega with the County Seal on the doors. Now his energies were more directed towards the renovation of our three-bedroom house. It went along coherently with his administrative work on commissioning the new Martin Luther King Jr Hospital and Charles Drew Medical School. Soon the USMC discipline was directed towards the five of us kids—The Crew.

For me, that meant being up at dawn, putting on a beanie, and learning to jog. It meant lists of chores tagged to the refrigerator. During the summer it meant "pop calls," when he would randomly appear during lunch to see whether or not we had swept the gutters, vacuumed the living room, shined his other shoes, cleaned the toilet, or made unauthorized use of his toolbox. It meant squat jumps as punishment. They were all about building upon the strengths of family and community. This, when there was no model.

No longer were the dreams of a Black Nation first and foremost. I'm sure he realized what massive coordination, money and discipline nation-building entailed just dealing with five hardheaded children and a hardheaded wife who found a different God and aimed at her own Master's degree.

Where he found any and all peace was in our camping spots, our hiking trails, and our favorite vistas up the Angeles Crest and Angeles Forest highways. Our 60-horsepower engine took the lot of us four boys out past Pasadena and the Rose Bowl, past Devil's Gate and Jet Propulsion Laboratory, through La Canada up to places named before us and named by us. We might go towards Red Box and up to the tunnel at Mt. Lowe, or the antennae at Mt. Wilson. We might stop at Clear Creek Station and hike to the lookout tower at Josephine Peak. We might try the axles on the dirt road to Wikiup or Valley Forge. We might head up to the top of Mt. Pacifico or maybe just have a chill picnic at Hidden Springs. The more remote and difficult to get there, the more we liked it.

We found an abandoned ski lift in a place we called Henry's Gulch. We bounded down a snowed-over firebreak on a hill we called Windy Gap. Chilao, the place with the visitor center, we studiously avoided. Charlton Flat? Well, that was just flat. The only time we enjoyed going to Switzer, the most popular spot, was when we hiked straight up the north face of the mountain, whereas everyone else hiked downstream to the waterfall. We considered ourselves hardcore; we outfitted ourselves from the army surplus store: cots, lanterns, tents, propane stove.

It was here that we could see Dad at rest. The campfire, the skillet of bacon, the old water pump at Valley Forge, miles east of the popular Red Box, reading books of poetry in the quiet crisp air—these were the comforts. But in order to enjoy these comforts, we had rules and we had responsibilities. We always hiked with the "Buddy System." You had to know where your buddy was at all times. You never left your buddy behind. You didn't shout to hear your own voice echo. You didn't throw rocks just to throw them. You didn't kick down loose objects to try and cause an avalanche. You didn't bring a radio. You didn't leave a trace of your having been there.

Over the years we encountered several rattlesnakes. We developed a drill called "Emergency In"—find your buddy and get to the bus. During the winter, we would pack as much snow as possible on the roof of the bus and bring it back to West Adams for snowball fights in the neighborhood. When we took neighborhood kids up, we would teach them the rules. When we encountered people on trails, we'd say "Howdy" and offer assistance if some was needed. We'd share food and water. By the time I was finishing high school, I knew dozens of sites and trails. I recognized in them the extent to which we recreated the best of our home life in the wilderness. We made the law, we defined the liberty, we shared our love of each other and of the land. This was our civilization under our control. We were peaceful stewards of the place.

Back at West Adams, we remade our house several times. We painted the stucco exterior avocado green. We sank poles and built fences. We replanted flowers. We placed bark in the middle of the two-track driveway. We trimmed the trees. We painted the garage a striking red, white, and blue for the Bicentennial. We expanded the patio by pouring cement. We built a two-story playhouse and also a tool shed. We painted and then paneled the hallway and bedrooms. We built bookshelves. We replaced windowpanes. We repurposed the garage theater into an office for my father and a bedroom for me.

It took a long time for all of the consequences of the way we lived to resonate against the negative assumptions about black Americans. The abstraction of transporting millions of people into change by a collective movement was something that could never be pinned down, but we knew where we could help. We knew where we could build. This life of service and growth showed me that the new black nation was within myself. It wasn't a destination for escape from America; it was an old part of America I could make new.

What this has made of me is an explorer. Born a Negro and raised to be Black, I then became an integration kid: a camper, a hiker, one who learned to change the wilderness into a home. My mythic metaphor for life is that I am from a small village surrounded by a dark forest. All of the elders and adults—save a few—live in mortal fear of the mysteries of that forest. I was born bold, and I ran deep into those woods and emerged changed. I told my people how I got my scar. "It was a bear. Follow me and I'll show you how to outwit the bear and see you to the other side." One dark forest has never been enough, and I have explored the plains and the mountains beyond. I never forget where I came from; I never shut up and I never stayed still. I have lived my life beyond the base camp of my Negro birth and Black adolescence. I am of the country. I am of the world. I have tamed the wilderness and lived beyond. All it took was courage, practice and dedication.

I often hear people struggling to find the "promised land." They sound lost, looking for a political solution. For us, in very understandable and practical ways, raising a family, working in service, keeping house, and climbing literal mountains demonstrated our ability to provide right where we stood. We embodied the promise so we could deliver that promise wherever we landed. There is no forest too dark nor trail too steep. The poet once said that "All that you have is your soul." I tell you, that is all you need.

II

A PERSONALIST PERSPECTIVE ON RESILIENCY

BY PHILLIP D. FLETCHER, PH.D.,
CITY OF HOPE OUTREACH

A resilient person is someone who has navigated difficult experiences maintaining the self. As a consequence, there is a change in perspective which occurs psychologically and emotionally enabling him or her to progress in life.

Suffering, if we allow the experience, can crush us under its emotional, psychological and physical weight. Every sphere of society, religious, political, social or economic, explicitly or implicitly works to mitigate the effects of suffering. Yet here is the other side to this coin: we can use suffering as an ally to improve our individual lives and our communities and establish a foundation for our children.

The last few years have offered American citizens an opportunity to conduct a period of self-reflection—if each of us takes that sacred moment to pause and look in the mirror. The Covid pandemic, protests, political divisions, economic stresses on households, and the stresses on interpersonal relationships have touched each of us to some degree.

We do not have to look very long to observe that human beings are distinct from other living beings, possessing a capacity to, across time and creation, influence life in extraordinary ways. Human beings develop relationships and create contributions to the world which are impactful and revolutionary.

John H. Crosby, in his work *The Personalism of John Paul II*,[87] reflects on human beings as belonging to themselves and having the capacity to determine in freedom who they shall be. "Persons are not just there, like rocks or plants; they are handed over to themselves, they can accept or reject themselves.... Above all, they can determine themselves in freedom, indeed, in a certain sense, they can create themselves."

Human persons—men and women created in the image of God—are radically different than the objects they have created for personal and societal usage. By belonging first to themselves, they have the intelligence and reason to determine how to respond to circumstances, establish relationships, and contribute to a home, a community, and the world. These acts should occur in the context of freedom, with an eye to the man or woman becoming his or her best future self. This establishes a fundamental truth in the philosophy of Personalism: Human persons, as subjects with dignity, possess the capacity to freely choose, rather than just exist as instruments which are used to accomplish a particular end.

As a philosophy, Personalism is not a new idea or wisdom; its roots are found in Christian doctrine as well as non-theistic works. In fact, its impact has been significantly felt in our own national development, both interpersonally and legislatively.

---

[87]   John H. Crosby, *The Personalism of John Paul II* (Hildebrand Press, 2019).

Reverend Dr. Martin L. King, Jr. (1929-1968) was an ardent proponent of Personalism, which he learned at Boston University. He applied its wisdom to his ministry and eventual Civil Rights leadership. King's application of Personalism to the Civil Rights Movement produced the idea the measurement of a man or woman is found in character, not phenotypic characteristics. Then he assembled a diversity of Americans—across ethnic, economic, religious, and political backgrounds—to march for equality before the law, securing legislation such as the 1964 Civil Rights Act and the 1965 Voting Rights Act.

Throughout the challenges of the Civil Rights Movement, King consistently articulated the Personalist idea of subjectivity to the human person, as one of the fundamental truths, to announce the brotherhood of Americans specifically, and humanity worldwide. He applied it to navigate the long road of objectification and dehumanization of Black Americans; both Black Americans and White Americans were called on to no longer view one another as animals or the embodiment of all that was evil, as expressed in racism and segregation. The objectification of human persons led to slavery, Jim Crow and segregation. King called on Americans to view one another as subjects: human persons capable of accomplishing individual and collective feats. The full recognition of human persons, regardless of ethnicity, possessing the freedom and the ability to become someone greater, was a consequence of King's Personalism. It was this perspective which guided the journey down the long road towards a better life for all Americans.

Finally, freedom is necessary to understand how to overcome difficulty to become our best future selves. Our world is fraught with situations like natural disasters, gun violence, illness, or car accidents, that act upon the human person. We face the realities of the unequal application of legislation and unwelcome business interests in communities.

The human person can rightly feel as if the world has determined to suffocate or extinguish his or her existence. There is indeed an emotional and psychological reaction manifesting as anger, depression, isolation, or despondency. These are human reactions to difficulties, and this necessitates empathy. At the same time, the human person—whose dignity is ineffable and reflects a transcendent being—has the freedom to either remain in a negative emotional and psychological state, or to act as a subject to move through the difficulty. The acting-through oneself is the actualization of resiliency. She is acknowledging the peculiar difficulty freely choosing to move forward—not as a consequence of coercion. Instead, she has recognized in herself the capacity to progress into someone greater.

A resilient person is someone who has navigated difficult experiences maintaining the self. As a consequence, there is a psychological and emotional change in perspective which enables the person to progress in life.

There are persons and communities within every locality which face social, economic and emotional challenges. The difficult experiences and environments offer opportunities either to shrink in the presence of these stresses or find avenues to negotiate and celebrate triumph. The stresses are more visible and shocking because resources to either hide or bring these difficulties to a quick end are minimal to nonexistent.

Considering the reality that there are persons and communities with limited resources, the journey towards resiliency must first include enduring the various hassles and major life events creatively, serving individuals and communities by stimulating minds, and increasing the capacity to recover from difficult conditions—if those stressors are viewed from a particular perspective.

Epictetus (c. 50 – c. 130 CE), a former slave and Stoic philosopher in ancient Greece, maintained that an individual possessed the power of choice regarding responses to life's difficult situations. In his summary wisdom titled, *Discourses*, he states, "You can bind up my leg, but not even Zeus has the power to break my freedom of choice." A person's ability to emerge mature and triumphant because of hassles and obstacles can be understood by a change in perspective. Epictetus observed that a human being could view his or her situation not as a victim, but as one who still possesses human agency to respond to difficult circumstances.

Human persons and communities are doomed to face suffering. Although some difficulties are the consequence of individual choice, there are afflictions which are thrust upon persons and communities, binding their ability to move forward and flourish. Epictetus, who himself experienced slavery, offers a perspective which can aid in the development of resiliency. The binding is real; the handicapped individual's experiences cannot be ignored and should be assessed according to the best of his or her ability. But human persons are not rendered impotent in the presence of life's hassles but possess the freedom and power to choose a different response and endure. The former slave recognizes obstacles and divine powers are impotent to eradicate an individual's ability to respond with courage and take one more step forward in life.

Resiliency does not have to occur in isolation. Human persons thrive in the context of social relationships, and opportunities to acquire wisdom, secure resources, and accomplish personal goals have a higher possibility of success within those relationships. In 2007, I established a nonprofit, The City of Hope Outreach (CoHO), to support the dignity of human persons who live in low-income situations, experience homelessness, and simply need an opportunity to thrive. Now in our sixteenth year, we have seen the importance of standing alongside individuals and families who are facing difficult situations related to education, housing and nutrition. There are men and women who have faced difficult odds daily and have found ways to negotiate those odds to secure a better future for themselves and children.

I am reminded of Adam, a homeless single father released from the Arkansas Department of Corrections. Adam became a resident of our CoHO Hope Home, which provides housing, and employment and financial assistance, to men who are pursuing a better life. Over the course of a two-year period—a long journey of case management, payment of fines, and employment training—Adam graduated from the CoHO Hope Home with his fines paid, his employment supporting men who were in need of the same assistance that he previously required. He is now also reunited with his daughter. Adam had to face the long journey of reclaiming his independence as well as integrating his past failures into his own life to secure a better future—a future which included a healing relationship between father and daughter.

Resiliency is not isolated to men and women who have no resources such as housing or other basic needs. Resiliency can be located in the life of a single mother like Rose, who carries the load of homemaker, employee, and student, as well as the role of both mother and father to her children. Rose became involved with CoHO simply to give back to others. There can be the perception single mothers do not have the time nor the power to look beyond their own circumstance—women viewed as victims of circumstance because they are left to serve as mother and father in the life of a child. Rose embodied the truth Epictetus spoke generations earlier. In what I would consider acts of defiance to the handicap of single parenting, she made decisions to respond differently to her difficulties. Rose was provided mentorship and offered resources to secure a college education while maintaining full employment and managing a home life. She exemplifies thousands of other single mothers in communities across our nation who are blooming out of concrete—women deciding to act with determination and humility and deciding to act with a different perspective and become better human persons for themselves and their children. Adam and Rose embody a resiliency which exemplifies the majesty of human dignity and freedom present in every human person.

A recognition of personhood affirms a human being's capacity to act freely in the face of difficult circumstances and enables those persons and communities to overcome extraordinary obstacles to become their best selves. Our subjectivity is critical to human agency, reinforcing our capability to respond with dignity in the face of difficulty. Secondly, a change in perspective involves human persons exercising his or her will to respond in thought, word and deed in ways which communicate to the self, "I will not be overpowered or defeated by this obstacle. This hassle in life will not have the final word." Epictetus provides a valuable contribution regarding the development of a resilient individual and community. Epictetus, Adam and Rose embody resiliency, speaking loudly from the past and in the present day. They are resilient persons who remind us that no obstacles, regardless of degree or omnipotence, can shatter the freedom of men and women to freely choose endurance over apathy, progress over diminishment, and hope over despondency.

PART III:
THE
CHALLENGES

I

RACE, RESPONSIBILITY, AND THE RULE OF LAW

BY GLENN LOURY, PH.D.

We should be a constitutional order of law.
All of our people should stand equal before the
law. Their standing before the law must not,
in our republic, be allowed to become condi-
tioned on their racial identity. The neutrality
of the law is a bedrock of our civilization.

W e're confronted in the twenty-first century with a country that has rapidly changed in the last seventy-five years,
with immigration in large numbers. Tens of millions
of new Americans have come, mostly from non-European points
of origin.

As we near the quarter-century mark, the anti-racism activists
will have to come to grips somehow with the continued laggardly status of substantial portions of the African American community. They
are attempting to do so by rewriting the American historical narrative
to focus on slavery and post-Emancipation anti-black racism.

The Civil Rights Movement of 1945 to 1970—some call it the
Second Reconstruction—has created an environment in which the

continuing marginal status, along many dimensions of social well-being of African Americans, needs to be rationalized. We have a wealth disparity—well, slavery must be the cause. We have higher poverty rates, lower educational achievement, lower home ownership—well, slavery, slavery and Jim Crow. We have family structure issues. We have behavioral problems in our communities with our young people. We have an achievement gap in the educational sphere. We have prisons mainly overflowing with young black men. Well, it's slavery. Well, it's racism in the very American DNA—anti-black racism. (We have to say anti-black racism now because this narrative is meant to carve out a kind of exceptionalism for blacks.)

The temptation is to embrace an account of the country and of our place within it which memorializes and elevates to an almost theological level the historical injury done to our people: the contempt for the humanity of our people, the hatred of our people. This temptation is compelling for many—rather than seeing the country as what I think it objectively is—a beacon of freedom and hope to all humanity to people from every corner of the globe, one of unlimited possibility, where the place of African Americans within it is, on the whole, a very favorable endowment. We've been dealt a good hand here, not a bad hand. Rather than accept that reality, I think people take comfort in a different account and I think it's a pity. It's a pity both because it does not do justice to what's been achieved over the last nearly three centuries here on the North American continent—the creation of the United States of America with all its warts—and also because it teaches our young children, our young African American children, a lie about their country.

The Civil War was a watershed event in the history of this republic, resulting in the death of 600,000 people in a country of 30 million, and the emancipation of the slaves. I believe that Abolition, the movement—the moral movement abetted by institutions of liberty that permitted people to assemble and to express their views and ultimately to persuade their fellows—is much more emblematic of, or characteristic of, the essence of the American experiment than the fact of slavery itself. Centering slavery does a disservice to the greatness, to the world historic achievement, which was the creation of the United States of America. For that reason, I disagree with the spirit of *The 1619 Project*,[88] which holds racism to be the driving force of the founding of and all that happens in this country.

But how are we going to understand these disparities? If I say that parents need to raise their kids, if I say that the behavior, the violent behavior, the predatory criminal behavior of large numbers of black people walking around in American cities is substantially responsible for the large numbers who are incarcerated—those thoughts don't fit the anti-racist narrative. But why should we think that any outcome disfavorable to African Americans is, *ipso facto*, an indictment of society, when America is as diverse, as dynamic, as prosperous, and as full of opportunity as it is? Where in this accountancy of responsibility is the ball ever in our court? When are we going to be responsible for how we raise our children and what we do with the opportunities that are in front of us?

We can lose ourselves in this pipedream narrative about "systemic racism" if we want to, but the twenty-first century is not going to wait for anybody. While we are going around with our hand out, talking about what was done to our ancestors, other people are busy building businesses, building their families, building their homes, and creating their lives. They're not going to stand still for us. What do we want to see in 2050—a third, or 40 percent, of black people being wards of the state, who are dealt with through a special dispensation because of something that was done two hundred years before to our

---

[88] "The 1619 Project," *The New York Times Magazine*, ed. Hannah Nicole Jones, August 14, 2019, https://www.nytimes.com/interactive/2019/08/14/magazine/1619-america-slavery.html.

ancestors? When are we going to recognize that it's time to man-up and woman-up—to face the realities of life?

There's no guarantee anywhere that life is fair, and in the case of African Americans within the American context, life has been particularly unfair at many junctures. But I want to know what the program is here. So, I have my program. My program is: get busy and seize the opportunities that exist. They are plentiful. Let's stop bellyaching and man-up and woman-up. That's my argument. Let's get busy.

The potential damage of embracing the narrative of systemic racism is especially evident in the area of law enforcement. For instance, if there is a rule created to enforce order and the numbers of those going into jail are disparate, the rule will be withdrawn because it is "racist." This applies both in the case of policing and in the courts. But ironically, what it does is undermine the ability of the police to assure public safety. Insisting that people must ignore racial disparities in rates of criminal offending and intra-racial violence lest they risk being accused of racism, is an especially consequential "framing" move that I believe is ultimately not in the interest of black people.

Building the current movement for police reform in explicit and predominantly racial terms is a mistaken strategic choice that has had profound consequences. Cities ended up burning because of the way the killing of George Floyd was narrated. Yet twice as many whites as blacks are killed by police in the U.S. each year, many of them under some of the most egregiously unjustifiable circumstances which rival the most celebrated cases of black victimization.

When black children are the accidental victims of black-on-black disputes, they get no coverage from the media, from politicians, or from the anti-racist protestors. Those stories don't fit the powerful narrative of white supremacy.

Recently on *The Glenn Show* I interviewed Sylvia Bennett-Stone, leader of a movement called Voices of Black Mothers United (VBMU). Sylvia's nineteen-year-old daughter Krystal Joy and a friend were in their car at a gas station, when they were caught in the crossfire of a black-on-black dispute. A single bullet killed both young girls.

I asked Sylvia, "Why do we know the names of the mothers of Trayvon Brown, Eric Gardner, and George Floyd, and not your name?"

"Because no one can make money off my baby," she answered. "We are so desensitized to this kind of event. It's normal. But let a white policeman kill one of us, we can make money off that. Our names and faces can go on billboards across the nation. We stay on television. If a police officer kills a black teenager, the whole world wants to burn everything down."

When innocent children are injured or killed in black-vs.-black violence, Sylvia said, it gets almost no attention. "There could be two such killings in one night and no one pays attention, often even in the black community. After the initial sympathy, no one wants to hear mothers anymore. 'They should go home and be quiet. When is she going to stop?' they say."

Before Krystal's death Sylvia had been leader of a small nonprofit organization in Birmingham, Alabama, serving her low-income community with literacy training, self-esteem training, and other initiatives. She had been an affiliate of the Woodson Center (formerly known as the National Center for Neighborhood Enterprise), which works to empower grassroots groups in low-income areas that are working to develop solutions to the problems of their communities. After her daughter was killed, Sylvia and the Center recruited other mothers who had lost their children to violence to come together and share what they were doing to heal—their best practices. That was the beginning of Voices of Black Mothers United.

When VBMU learns that a mother has just lost a child to violence, Sylvia and other members who have had the same experience immediately go to the mother to give her comfort and love. They encourage the mother to go to the scene of the homicide to deal with the community and try to tone tempers down. "No mother wants another mother to lose her child because somebody wants to avenge the death through violent retaliation," Sylvia says. Then they talk about creating a project to bring some kind of safety to the community. "We give them purpose."

Through the Woodson Center, she and her organization also work with police in an effort led by former Charlottesville and Baltimore Police Chief Rodney Monroe. When a violent event occurs, the police need to get as much information as possible, and VBMU sets the tone to avoid retaliatory violence and escalation. They help the families, and they help the police do their jobs. The organization also works with the police to promote accountability and anti-discrimination initiatives within police departments.

Sylvia estimates that far from supporting a "De-Fund the Police" movement, 80 percent of people in minority communities would say they need the police. But those are not the voices we hear.

The members of VBMU group have each endured a terrible event—the loss of a child to violence. They have stepped up to the problem and are working to do something to keep violence from escalating, as so often has been the result. The destruction and burning that followed the killing of George Floyd resulted in economic losses and the suffering of thousands of black residents in cities all over the country.

What we have, in the face of the awful tragedy of losing a child, is a constructive response from the survivors of the victims—to take matters into their own hands and to try to move forward positively. Voices of Black Mothers United has grown, with state leaders around the country. They are focused on their mission, and they refuse to look at the world through the prism of race.

This is my belief: we should be a constitutional order of law. All of our people should stand equal before the law. Their standing before the law must not, in our republic, be allowed to become conditioned on their racial identity. The neutrality of the law is a bedrock of our civilization.

2

BUILD RESILIENCE AND AGENCY, NOT LOWER EXPECTATIONS AS THE PATHWAY TO TRIUMPH

BY IAN V. ROWE

What enables people of all races to overcome extraordinary obstacles, tragedy, and trauma? Is it the elimination of those obstacles, the objective standards? Or is it the resilient muscle that grows when you regularly encounter resistance?

"Don't inflict on us the consequences of a soft bigotry of low expectations. Don't presume that we're not capable of objectively expressing excellence in the same way as any other people are expressing excellence."[89] In 2019, in front of students and faculty at the College of the Holy Cross in Massachusetts, Brown University Professor and Economist Glenn

---

[89] Mark J. Perry, "Glenn Loury: 'Affirmative action is dishonest. It's not about equality, it's about covering ass'," *AEIdeas* (blog), June 21, 2019, https://www.aei.org/carpe-diem/glenn-loury-affirmative-action-is-dishonest-its-not-about-equality-its-about-covering-ass/.

Loury bluntly spoke on behalf of black Americans in response to the misguided agenda to achieve so-called "racial equity."

What sparked Loury's ire was an affirmative action scheme that patronized black people by judging them by different and lower standards to assess fitness for university life. The outrage could justifiably be pointed at any number of cynical steps intended to "preference" blacks supposedly incapable of succeeding on their own: abandonment of objective assessments like the SAT for college admission; elimination of deadlines to submit homework—if not removal of the requirement overall; ending of honors classes; relaxation of graduation requirements, and so on.

Two modern day examples illustrate the point:

- In New Jersey, in 2023, the state Board of Education voted to lower the minimum passing score on the state's high school graduation test. According to Chris Cerf, former superintendent of Newark Public Schools and the former New Jersey commissioner of education, "One board member who supported lowering the passing score suggested that it was 'unfair' to 'Black and Latino students' to require underperforming students to demonstrate a higher level of proficiency in reading and math before graduating."[90] Why would the school board so blatantly reduce the standard? Under the prior passing score, 39 percent of students would be "graduation ready" in reading. With the decision to reduce the required score, the numbers would leap to 80 percent in reading. Voila, student mastery achieved!

- On the other coast, in Culver City, California, members of the school board were frustrated that the high school honors

---

[90] Chris Cerf, "Ex-education commish: Lowering passing test scores is a parlor trick that hurts our kids," *NJ.com*, May 10, 2023, https://www.nj.com/opinion/2023/05/ex-education-commish-lowering-passing-test-scores-is-a-parlor-trick-that-hurts-our-kids-opinion.html.

English classes didn't enroll enough Black and Latino students. Rather than improve the preparation of these students during the elementary and middle school years, the school board—in the name of "racial equity"— simply eliminated the honors English classes in the ninth and tenth grades.[91] Don't like the demographic outcomes when you apply an objective standard that all students have to pass? Well, just remove the objective standard.

As someone who has for more than a decade run public charter schools in low-income communities in the Bronx, educating almost exclusively black and Hispanic students, I know the inspiring impact on students when expectations are raised, not dumbed down. Conversely, I have seen the debilitating effect on children when standards are shifted downward or removed in order to account for perceived racial deficits. With breathtaking speed, many institutions of higher education and K-12 schools have adopted a perverse social justice agenda that prioritizes cosmetic representation versus actual learning and achievement.

The logic tree for implementing these types of initiatives emerges from critical race theory and anti-racist dogma. Any assessment that reveals racial inequity in outcomes must itself—the theory goes—be racially biased, and thus inherently guilty of perpetuating those inequities. Therefore, the perverse logic concludes, it's best either to create a system of reverse racial discrimination or just to eliminate these so-called discriminatory measurements.

But is it best? This is the essential question the Woodson Center for the Study of Resilience seeks to answer: What enables people of all races to overcome extraordinary obstacles, tragedy and trauma? Is it the elimination of those obstacles, the objective standards? Or

---

[91]   Sara Randazzo, "To Increase Equity, School Districts Eliminate Honors Classes," *Wall Street Journal*, February 17, 2023, https://www.wsj.com/articles/to-increase-equity-school-districts-eliminate-honors-classes-d5985dee.

is it the resilient muscle that grows when you regularly encounter resistance?

Imagine a track and field meet featuring runners lined up to race the 100-meter hurdles. If a runner had trained only on an empty track, with no hurdles, would it be a surprise if he or she had not developed strength in the quadriceps, hip flexors, hamstrings, gluteus, and abdominal muscles that develop in those who had regularly practiced jumping drills?

The legendary tennis star Billie Jean King coined the phrase "Pressure is a privilege," when explaining how she was able to parlay high expectations for herself—and those of others—into becoming one of the greatest athletes of all time. Not only is pressure a privilege, there is a corollary. The *absence* of pressure—the lack of the responsibility to meet an objective standard—can also create a false sense of achievement. Winning a 100-meter race in which all the competitors except you have to leap over hurdles would be a hollow victory, with the added sting that everyone else would know you did not earn the prize on a level playing field.

In urban education, a common practice that too often produces similar "hollow victories," and adversely affects primarily low-income black boys, is social promotion. Social promotion occurs when a student is moved from one grade to the next grade, regardless of whether that student has mastered the grade level material. This practice of moving unprepared kids up in the early grades has especially cruel consequences as the student ages.

According to the National Center for Education Statistics,[92] in 2015 only 18 percent of fourth grade black students were reading at or above the Proficient level defined by the National Assessment for

---

[92] "Table 221.20, Percentage of students at or above selected National Assessment of Educational Progress (NAEP) reading achievement levels, by grade and selected student characteristics: Selected years, 2005 through 2019," National Center for Education Statistics, https://nces.ed.gov/programs/digest/d19/tables/dt19_221.20.asp

Educational Progress (aka the Nation's Report Card). The same analysis shows that in 2019, only 15 percent of that *same* cohort of black students, now in eighth grade, were reading at or above the NAEP Proficient levels.

Is it any wonder then that we see this result in a study featured in a report: "Should We End Social Promotion? Truth and Consequences: By the time the students reach the ages of fifteen to seventeen, 50 percent of African American boys are either below the grade of their peers that age or have dropped out of school."[93]

The reasons for the poor performance of these students are myriad, including less access to high quality schools and more unstable families. But despite those challenges, when standards are reduced—in this case lowering the criteria for grade promotion—then we rob young people, in the most challenging circumstances, of the objective measure that would force teachers and students to work together to ensure students meet those measures.

What these perhaps well-intentioned, but certainly misguided, efforts add up to is an anti-meritocratic assault on black agency and resiliency. It is a choice. In that Culver City, CA district that eliminated the honors English class, the Superintendent Quoc Tran made a revealing confession: "It was very jarring when teachers looked at their AP enrollment and realized black and brown kids were not there. They felt obligated to do something."[94] Yes, let's do *something*. But that thing has to be to raise expectations and provide the support to help students meet them. This district opted for exactly the opposite, by eliminating the program altogether.

---

[93] Robert M. Hauser, "Should We End Social Promotion? Truth and Consequences," Center for Demography and Ecology, The University of Wisconsin-Madison, May 20, 2017, https://cde.wisc.edu/wp-content/uploads/sites/839/2019/01/cde-working-paper-1999-06.pdf.

[94] Emma Camp, "To Increase 'Equity,' This California High School Is Eliminating Honors Courses," *Reason*, 2.21.2023, https://reason.com/2023/02/21/to-increase-equity-this-california-high-school-is-eliminating-honors- courses/.

What makes all of this bar-lowering so appalling is that it completely ignores the story of the African American experience in the United States, filled with heroic tales of dogged perseverance, even in the face of discriminatory laws and attitudes in a nation guilty of the original sin of slavery.

A great place to learn these stories is in the Woodson Center's K-12 Black History and Character Curriculum, which is based on the ten Woodson Principles: Competence, Integrity, Transparency, Resilience, Witness, Innovation, Inspiration, Agency, Access, and Grace.[95]

The curriculum tells the stories of black Americans whose tenacity and resilience enabled them to overcome adversity and make invaluable contributions to our country. It also teaches character and decision-making skills that equip students to take charge of their futures. The curriculum—free and publicly available for all—has now been downloaded more than a hundred thousand times by teachers and parents in all fifty states, exposing young people of all races to numerous instances of triumph over adversity.

Even beyond this curriculum, many examples of black excellence abound. The educator Marva Collins trained more than one hundred thousand teachers, principals, and administrators in the methodology developed and practiced at her Westside Preparatory School in one of the poorest districts in Chicago.

"For thirty years, we have done what other schools declare impossible," explains Collins. "I don't make excuses—I take responsibility. If children fail, it's about me, not them. I tell my students, if you think excellence is difficult, you don't want to try failure."[96]

---

95   The Woodson Center, "Curriculum," https://woodsoncenter.org/how-we-help/curriculum/.

96   National Endowment for the Humanities, "Marva Collins, "National Humanities Medal—2004," https://www.neh.gov/about/awards/national-humanities-medals/marva-collins.

As a way to instill self-worth, each morning at Westside Preparatory, students began with a recitation known as the creed: twenty-two verses that stress positive thinking, responsibility, and achievement as individual choices. The core curriculum emphasized phonics, reading, English, math, and classics, with a reading list that included Sophocles, Homer, Plato, Chaucer, and Tolstoy.

According to Collins, "Values can be replicated, excellence can be replicated, but it has to begin with the idea that everything is about me, not the other person, and about being proud of my work."

For her work, in 2004 Marva Collins was awarded the National Humanities Medal, an honor bestowed by the National Endowment for the Humanities to individuals whose work has deepened the nation's understanding of the humanities and broadened our citizens' engagement with history, literature, languages, philosophy, and other humanities subjects.

Imagine if every educator demanded this high level of expectation for students of all races, and not what we see too often today: leaders within the private, public, and philanthropic sectors becoming self-anointed agents of social justice, lowering the bar of achievement.

With the 2023 Supreme Court decision to strike down race-based affirmative action in college admissions, there is now a unique opportunity to refocus our efforts on merit and strengthen outcomes for not only black, but all students in the K-12 education system. In his majority opinion, Chief Justice John Roberts wrote, "Many universities have for too long wrongly concluded that the touchstone of an individual's identity is not challenges bested, skills built or lessons learned, but the color of their skin.... This Nation's constitutional history does not tolerate that choice."

Years from now, black students admitted to top schools will say, "Thank you, Supreme Court, for a decision that removes the perception that the only reason I got in is due to my race." You can hear echoes of Glenn Loury's declaration that when the objective standard is removed, so is the mechanism to prove competence against that objective standard.

Indeed, at a time when it takes courage to speak obvious truths, Loury's plea to all of us is to call out this agenda for what it is—a taking away of the level playing field that black Americans have historically sought to demolish stereotypes of inferiority and to prove our ability to compete at the highest levels. It does not have to be this way.

Perhaps Supreme Court Justice Clarence Thomas summarized it best as he wrote in his concurring opinion.[97] "The solution to our Nation's racial problems cannot come from policies grounded in affirmative action or some other conception of equity," Thomas writes. "Racialism simply cannot be undone by different or more racialism. Instead, the solution announced in the second founding is incorporated in our Constitution: that we are all equal and should be treated equally before the law without regard to our race," he adds. "Only that promise can allow us to look past our differing skin colors."

Let us fulfill that promise by forging a path forward marked by hope and agency, not grievance and dependency. Let us re-establish merit as the core criterion to be considered against a standard bar of excellence. The rising generation of black children and young people of all races deserve the opportunity to rise or fall *fairly*—and with the equal chance to build resiliency in each effort to succeed.

---

[97] Spencer Brown, "Clarence Thomas' Concurring Opinion on Affirmative Action Is Incredible," *Townhall*, June 29, 2023, https://townhall.com/tipsheet/spencerbrown/2023/06/29/clarence-thomas-opinion-in-affirmative-action-case-is-a-work-of-art-n2625132.

3

OF FIREFLIES AND SECOND TRIES, SELF-RELIANCE OR SOCIAL JUSTICE: THE SECOND RECONSTRUCTION

BY JANICE ROGERS BROWN, J. D., LL.M.,
RETIRED CIRCUIT JUDGE

*In the 1960s, our cultural and political ethic
shifted from personal responsibility and self-
determination to therapeutic alienation. The
message of the Voting Rights Act was, "If you are
trying to join the political community, we will
remove obstacles." Meanwhile, the Great Society
absorbed the countercultural mood and conceded: "If
you are acting up, vowing to destroy the political
community, you may be entitled to tribute."*

I was born in Alabama, in a little town called Greenville in Butler County. I know it was Butler County because it says so on my birth certificate, but I don't think I spent any other time there. Until I was about eight years old, I lived in Crenshaw County, in an even smaller town called Luverne. As a small child growing up in the bosom of a loving and protective family, I had a pretty idyllic childhood. I roamed freely in the piney woods, ate berries ripe from the bush, and made firefly lanterns, which to my dismay never lasted very long. I trudged barefoot along the dusty roads and dreamed the sweet, innocent, heroic dreams that all children dream. I loved the summer lightning that raised the fine hairs on the back of my neck and those pitch black nights without the benefit of streetlights, when the dense thicket of stars wheeled above my head in such wonderful profusion that I lost all sense of being earthbound. I crossed the cosmos with fifty-meter strides and swam laps in the Milky Way.

By today's standards, my early experiences were circumstances of material deprivation. We were poor, especially my mother's family. Her father supported a wife and seven children, cropping shares in the summer and driving a logging truck over treacherous, mud-slick roads in the winter. The family moved every year from one pine-board, tin-roofed shack to another. When I came to visit in the summers, my aunt and I often shared a pallet on the floor, and through the rust holes in the roof, we were showered with starlight. Of course, rain was even more entertaining. Then the challenge was to find enough containers to capture all the drips. My grandfather's harmonica sometimes mimicked the driving wheels of passing trains; other times I heard the receding wails of a locomotive rushing past southern crossings in the waiting dark. Sometimes my mother's younger brothers made a percussion instrument of their denim-covered legs, flexing and flicking the fingers of one hand along their thighs, incorporating the syncopated rhythms of falling water.

My father's family was comparatively well-off. His parents owned a few acres of land. I am sure their annual income would have put them well below anybody's idea of a poverty level, but that was of little consequence. It was a time and place where what you had mattered much less than the kind of person you were. A person's worth was not measured in BMWs, Gucci bags, and imported espresso machines.

There was no moral relativism practiced in the homes where I spent my childhood. There was right and wrong, good and evil. It was a stern southern Christian upbringing; fear God and seek understanding was the watchword. We went to church twice on Sundays, and again on Wednesday. A certain mental and physical toughness was expected. The rules for life were uncomplicated: "Don't lie, don't cheat, don't steal, don't beg, and don't envy. And whatever you do—don't snivel. Keep your word. Work hard. Strive for excellence. Do unto others...even when they don't do the same unto you."

But there was an ominous and insistent theme that ran beneath my seemingly carefree childhood—something I hardly understood but deeply felt. There was an alertness in the air like the first smell of smoke from a distant fire. Despite the fact that our roots were many generations deep, we were not quite welcome and not quite citizens. Though we were comforting and familiar, we were also alien and despised.

It was a peculiar existence with austere rules. I attended a Black church and a segregated school. I never drank from the colored fountain, used the colored restroom, or sat in the colored waiting room at the bus station, and I certainly never went to see a movie where I would be relegated to the colored balcony—which meant I never went to the movies at all. A large part of my young life was structured to avoid these indignities. If we traveled, we packed a hearty lunch. We waited outside the bus station or the train depot until it was time to board.

Long after leaving the deep South, we still had rules. When we returned for a visit, we made the drive without taking in the view at any scenic overlooks or stopping for coffee or pausing to sleep. The wheels of our car never stopped turning in Mississippi. We felt marginally safer in Alabama, but not much. It was home. We knew the backroads and the short cuts. I spent many evenings sitting on the porch, listening to my uncles tell of harrowing escapes: being shadowed all the way to the state line by a car following too closely, high beams throwing a blinding haze in the rear-view mirror. I adored my uncles—men who wore sharp suits, rakishly tilted hats, and had beautifully shined shoes. They had gone "North" to work in the auto plants and traded their cars every couple of years. They believed in the value of well-tuned V-8 engines. They knew those engines would not outrun bullets, and yet they sat in the darkness, recalling their adventures, their smiles gentle, their voices teasing. No doubt that is why I still have a soft spot for muscle cars and sharp-dressed men.

In the 1940s, Woodie Guthrie sang: "This land is your land, and this land is my land." In the Alabama of the '40s and '50s, it wasn't necessarily so. On the surface, race relations in Alabama seemed quiescent. The high tide of vigilantism, paramilitary exploits, and lynch law had receded, though it had not been extinguished. Although the valor of black soldiers fighting to preserve the Union convinced some people that black soldiers at least had earned the right to be welcomed into the political community, in the South, a black man in uniform remained an intolerable affront. Black veterans of The Great War and World War II demanded to be given at home the rights they had fought for overseas. White resistance to those demands returned lynchings to the headlines. Mobs assassinated "no fewer than six war veterans in a single three-week period in the summer of 1946."[98] With America smarting from accusations of hypocrisy leveled by Asian and African peoples, Truman appointed a commission to investigate racial unrest and sent a special message to Congress asking for federal

---

[98] Taylor Branch, *Parting the Waters: America in the King Years 1954-63* (New York: Simon & Schuster 1988), 63.

anti-lynching legislation.[99] The bill went nowhere, but the effort brought "civil rights" into "common political parlance."[100]

Compulsory segregation and the Southern Way of Life were abstractions that did not much trouble the conscience of most northern whites, especially since they accomplished *de facto* what Jim Crow mandated. A sort of cruel dhimmitude for black Americans became the comfortable norm, both above and below the Mason-Dixon line. As Alexander Bickel acknowledged, "Segregation had prospered and come to full flower at least partly in reliance upon the Court's decision, in 1896, that it conformed to constitutional principle."[101]

After the Supreme Court declared in *Brown* that "separate was inherently unequal," Alabama, along with a broad swath of the other southern states, responded with massive resistance. *Brown*, now at the core of the constitutional canon, did not overrule *Plessy*'s separate but equal doctrine. The decision ignored constitutional exegesis in favor of sociological vignettes. And it "crystalize [d] southern resistance to social change."[102] White Citizen's Councils proliferated, but so did protests and demonstrations by Black Southerners determined to resist the continuation of business as usual. The Councils, cannily attempting to claim the moral high ground, nominally eschewed violence, but openly "adopted a policy of harsh economic reprisals against Negroes who fought segregation."[103] Integration, they insisted, was a moral outrage.

On the eve of the Montgomery bus boycott, which began while Alabama officials were still smarting from the *Brown* decision, Reverend King voiced centuries of inchoate longing when he

---

99 Ibid.
100 Ibid.
101 Alexander M. Bickel, *The Least Dangerous Branch: The Supreme Court at the Bar of Politics,* (New Haven: Yale University Press 1962), 249.
102 Michael J. Klarman, "How Brown Changed Race Relations: The Backlash Thesis," *The Journal of American History*, Vol. 81, Issue 1 June 1994, 81-82.
103 Branch. *Parting the Waters*, 138.

declared, "There comes a time when people get tired of being thrown across the abyss of humiliation." He asked the thousands who filled and overflowed the Holt Street Baptist Church if they "had the moral courage to stand up for their rights;" to work "with grim and bold determination" to gain justice. He assured them their pursuit of justice was not wrong. "If we are wrong," he said, "the Supreme Court is wrong. If we are wrong, God Almighty is wrong. If we are wrong—Jesus of Nazareth was merely a utopian dreamer and never came down to earth. If we are wrong—justice is a lie."[104]

That meeting, convened by the First Montgomery Improvement Association (MIA)—an organization Ms. Rosa Parks served as secretary—occurred just five days after her arrest. By December 1956, boycotters had brought the Montgomery transit system to the brink of insolvency, and a federal court declared, in *Browder v. Gayle*, that the segregation of public transit was unconstitutional.

Despite the Supreme Court's disappointing decision in 1903, Jackson Giles' Colored Man's Suffrage Association did not give up the fight. Fifty years later, there were Improvement Associations and Civic Associations all over Alabama. Dr. King established the Southern Christian Leadership Conference (SCLC) to focus on access to the ballot, but lacking any grassroots organization to augment his efforts and hampered by various rivalries and jealousies among organizations that might have been allies, SCLC was less effective than it might have been. Despite generally enthusiastic and well-attended rallies, and the momentum provided by a high-profile Children's Crusade,[105] the effort produced negligible increases in registration. Restoring the franchise was a long, slow, arduous process.

Other less trendy, long-established efforts began to bear fruit. Before the Department of Justice's Civil Rights Division had even

---

[104]   Ibid. 140-41.
[105]   Janice Kelsey, *I Woke Up With My Mind on Freedom* (Pittsburgh: Urban Press, 2017), 12-13, 22-23.

started its work, civic improvement associations like the MIA were holding voter registration drives, and not just by dispersing people with clipboards to every street corner or store front. In those days, it required courage and stamina for a Black citizen to apply for voter registration in Alabama. The odds were good you wouldn't get to vote, but even worse, you might lose your livelihood, be threatened, assaulted, or even killed. Neither physical and economic terrorism, nor procedural and logistical obstacles, exhausted the committed segregationists' options for obstruction.

Despite serious threats of retaliation, the ubiquitous civic associations had to encourage and persuade people to apply. Then, the association gathered information: where is the registrar going to be next week; what is the information on the questionnaire, what questions tripped people up in the past. The organizations' volunteers coached applicants with the right answers so they could answer the trick questions. When the disenfranchised registrants got discouraged, the civic associations were there to push them to try again. In Crenshaw County where I spent my childhood, there was a voting age population of roughly eighty-five hundred, about 75 percent of them White.[106] In 1964, 86 percent of the White voting age population was registered to vote, compared to only 22 percent of similarly situated Black residents—that is, just under five hundred people. And that number represented a big increase from 1954.

The obstacles a Black resident faced in trying to register in Alabama were daunting: The registrars would move around and not publicize where they were receiving applications. They would require an applicant to have another registered voter vouch for the applicant's identity and maybe even to his or her good character. Usually, the person vouching had to be White. The registrars required applicants to fill out complicated questionnaires, full of trick questions on the

---

[106] Dept. of Justice Status Report quoting Voting Rights: Hearing Before the Senate Committee on the Judiciary, 89th Cong. 1327 (1965). 168.

Constitution and the government, phrased with double and *triple* negatives. If you were White, the registrar would fill it out for you. If you were Black, you had to fill it out—flawlessly—on your own.[107] Of course, these were only the procedural and logistical obstacles.

The federal government made two attempts to secure Black citizens the vote before the 1965 Act. Under those earlier statutes, the Department of Justice brought suit in federal courts in southern states, and the residents' persistent attempts to register became valuable evidence in those lawsuits. They also showed what was wrong with the system as it stood. As one barrier to Black registration weakened—for example, simple literacy tests—the states erected others. Voter registration was a moving target, and it was moving too fast for litigation to effectively counter. A court could enjoin one kind of qualification for voting, only to see another different qualification replace it. Organizations like the civic associations, continuing to press for registration, exposed each new qualification as it arose.

The pre-1965 acts were heavily dependent on judicial integrity and independence. For example, the 1960 Act required a federal judge to appoint a federal referee to supervise registration if the evidence proved a county had denied its Black citizens the right to vote. That sounded promising; A judge could find an honest referee to apply the law impartially. In practice, however, judges faced enormous social pressure to deter any threat to Southern white autonomy. Thus, it was not surprising that judges often appointed referees who were less fair than the registrars had been—nor that other judges would grant only the most grudging partial relief, doing no more for enfranchisement

---

[107]   Caldwell, Christopher. The Age of Entitlement (New York: Simon & Schuster, 2020). 12. Caldwell explains how Fulton County, Georgia kept black people from voting "by requiring them to complete a 30-item questionnaire demanding that they lay out the bureaucratic procedure for changing the seat of a county, name the state comptroller and all the state's federal district court judges, and state how many votes Georgia had in the federal electoral college."

than the law absolutely clearly required. The pre-1965 voting rights movement demonstrated the folly of poor institutional design.

The Founders believed the federal government should be strictly limited to its enumerated powers. The Constitution was drafted to instantiate those limits. Of course, the Civil War, and the constitutional amendments which resulted from it, changed forever the relationship between the federal government and the states. The Voting Rights Act is an example of federal power at its most intrusive. Until recently, in states like Alabama, the VRA gave the U.S. Department of Justice absolute authority over the conduct of state and local *elections*, the heart of local democracy. The preclearance process was burdensome and expensive, and officials in covered localities resented it.

So why was not the Voting Rights Act anathema to those who favored the Founder's constitution? A surprisingly broad consensus supported the VRA as an example of good federal intervention. Ordinarily, conservatives condemn all expansions of government as bad. And Libertarians insist the idea of good government intrusion is oxymoronic. If there is such a thing as salutary government intervention, is it possible to identify it and differentiate it from the relentless overreaching of the administrative state? A comparison between the Voting Rights Act with some of the "Great Society" programs, enacted about the same time, is instructive. There are significant differences.

The folks in Alabama who sought the right to vote were not just the heirs of Jackson Giles. Like black people all over the south, they sought not only to cash in the long overdue promissory note proffered in the Declaration of Independence, but to prove themselves the deserving beneficiaries of the black men who fought to preserve the Union even before its flag belonged to them. Moreover, were they not entitled to demand that the descendants of the defeated rebels, who pledged themselves to a law-abiding peace, finally fulfill that commitment?

Second, the Voting Rights Act does have a textual basis in the Constitution. The Fifteenth Amendment states that "the right of citizens of the United States to vote shall not be denied or abridged... by any State on account of race." And the Fourteenth Amendment mandates equal protection of the laws.

Third, the Voting Rights Act was a response to the constant and diligent effort of citizens to claim their rights. When all that they could do was not enough, the federal government intervened. Fourth, the drafters of the Voting Rights Act, based on actual experience, carefully crafted the features of the final legislation for implementation by ordinary humans.

At least one Alabama newspaper speculated that law enforcement's over-reaction to the Selma-to-Montgomery March in 1965 was the primary impetus for the VRA: "The harsh and extravagant voting rights bill was passed...at the Edmund Pettus Bridge, when Col. Lingo's forces of law and order commenced to beat the daylights out of a handful of marchers. The television view of that cruel and stupid performance brought...new shame to the state.... Mark it well: Alabama passed this law."

That may have been a bit of an exaggeration. By the time mounted officers—wielding clubs made of pieces of old tires studded with metal spikes—clashed with demonstrators on the bridge, Black Americans had already refuted every claim that purportedly made them ineligible to exercise the franchise, demonstrating their "capacity for education, creative achievement, and a phenomenal gift for self-discipline in the face of the white man's humiliations in both the North and the South."[108] The public had seen Norman Rockwell's evocative portrait of Ruby Bridges' first day of school; they had heard the soaring cadences of Martin Luther King's "I have a Dream" speech; the camera's unblinking eye had allowed the nation to watch

---

[108] Fawn Brodie, *Thaddeus Stevens: Scourge of the South* (New York: W. W. Norton & Co., 1966), 373.

grown men and women, confronting, cursing, hurling racial invectives and other missiles at a small band of "scrubbed, starched, scared and incredibly brave [black] children."[109] The existence of a permanently disenfranchised, disfavored caste made a mockery of America's claim of freedom and equality. Meanwhile, the State Department was using jazz musicians—like Louie Armstrong, Dizzy Gillespie, Dave Brubeck, and Benny Goodman—as weapons in the Cold War, to tip the balance in a "fierce competition to win hearts and minds" internationally. Although some of the musicians grew up in the Jim Crow South, jazz was touted as the perfect metaphor for America; the "music of democracy and freedom," and the multi-racial bands projected an image of racial harmony[110] that violent assaults on non-violent demonstrators contradicted. When Dizzy Gillespie left on his first sponsored tour, The *New York Times* proclaimed, "America's secret weapon is a blue note in a minor key." The people had struggled to make sense of the televised murder of a President, as well as the televised murder of his alleged assailant. They were told that delivering the *coup de grace* to Jim Crow was a fitting way to memorialize their martyred leader.[111] And with the impassioned speeches of Nuremberg ringing in their ears in their own living rooms, in flickering black and white images, they saw the mean, hateful, unjust reality of second-class citizenship.

Thus, it is likely the confrontation on the Edmund Pettus bridge merely hastened what had already become an inevitability.

---

109 Bickel, *The Least Dangerous Branch*, 267.
110 Billy Perrigo, "How the U.S. Used Jazz as a Cold War Secret Weapon," *Time*, December 22, 2017.
111 Christopher Caldwell, *Age of Entitlement* (New York: Simon & Shuster, 2020), 4, 8-9.

Every Goodbye Ain't Gone

Black residents of Crenshaw and other counties were entitled to vote, and they demanded specifically that. They demanded access to the ballot, and they did everything possible within the law to achieve that right. In these circumstances, the Voting Rights Act of 1965, including the Section 5 preclearance procedure, was justified.

Compare this story to the "War on Poverty." Both programs became firmly established in the 1960s. To many people they seemed to represent two parts of the same response. In reality, they represent two sides of a significant discontinuity. The Voting Rights Act was the end of one paradigm, the Great Society the first undertaking of a new one. Those who brought about the final resolution of the Voting Rights Act were civilly disobedient activists who accepted the consequences of their disobedience. They were committed to the rule of law and determined to work within the system to change it. The impetus for the War on Poverty arose from the theories of academics—never tested on the ground—and the deal was sealed by explosions of violence in Newark, Los Angeles, Detroit, Chicago, and Washington D.C. The rioters in America's ghettos, and later on its elite college campuses, were not committing themselves to American ideals and seeking an equal opportunity to participate. They were repudiating those ideals. The Great Society may have mollified them, but at huge costs, both financial and social. In Washington, D.C. more than fifty years later, neighborhoods destroyed by ancient riots are still trying to recover their community character. Block after block of "projects" stand empty, their blank windows the only sentinels to empty fields of debris.

In the 1960s, our cultural and political ethic shifted from personal responsibility and self-determination to therapeutic alienation.[112] The

---

[112]   This helpful phrase is courtesy of John McWhorter, *Winning the Race: Beyond the Crisis in Black America* (New York: Penguin 2006), 153-197.

message of the Voting Rights Act was, "If you are trying to join the political community, we will remove obstacles." Meanwhile, the Great Society absorbed the countercultural mood and conceded: "If you are acting up, vowing to destroy the political community, you may be entitled to tribute." Of course, nothing is quite that simple. Suffice it to say that the Voting Rights Act was a resounding success, so much so that in 2007 Mississippi produced the first case in which a court determined a Black election official had diluted the votes of his white constituents.[113] But the War on Poverty has been a dismal failure. The seedy ghettos of the 1960s became the urban killing fields of the 1990s. Not even the most optimistic proponents of these programs can claim things are getting better.

The 1965 Voting Rights Act did well to put power and responsibility in the Department of Justice. So far as that goes, it sounds like the Great Society programs—for every problem there is an administrative agency to solve it. However, there are critical differences in the incentives the Voting Rights Act provides. For one thing, a state or locality can free itself from the requirement of preclearance. To do so, it has to show that it has extended the franchise fairly, without discrimination, for at least ten years.[114] That is a proper incentive— if a state demonstrates its compliance, the federal intervention will end. By contrast, programs in the Great Society never end, they only expand. States are dependent now on federal funding of welfare programs, Medicaid, education, and so on. Another difference is that the initial Voting Rights Act left the ultimate responsibility to individuals to claim their rights. The federal government did not guarantee success at the polls, and it did not (as many states do now) automatically register people who show up to obtain some unrelated government service, e.g., to register their vehicle. The VRA removed obstacles to registration, guaranteeing an equal opportunity for everybody to

---

[113]   United States v. Brown (S.D. Miss. 2007) 494 F.Supp.2d 440.
[114]   42 U.S.C. § 1973b(a).

participate in politics, and each person was responsible for completing the process. It did not attempt, like the Great Society programs did, to guarantee equal results.

When the government responds to the focused efforts of its citizens; when it helps those people who have done everything they can to help themselves; when it acts in such a way that it increases their incentives to keep working for themselves, then federal intervention can protect liberty, rather than destroy it. The goal is to encourage, rather than undermine, private activity.

The compound failures of freedom gave birth to jazz, a supple, sumptuous, untethered sound that skims the soft tendrils of the soul and feels like a dream of flying. The anthem of The Great Society is always a scream of rage.

Faith and Courage

Dostoevsky declares that beauty will save the world, because beauty, truth, and the good comprise a unity. Truth and freedom live and die together. Truth cannot be defended without courage. There is no courage without faith. And no faith without humility. "Fear of the mob" [] is "an ambiguous feeling...more easily satisfied...by conceding what the mob wants...than by fighting it."[115] Once, the civil rights struggle owned a moral valence. Communities of faith, exhorted by their leaders, many of whom were ministers, were taught the moral courage to face the mob. Now, the race hustlers and charlatans who wrap themselves in the mantle of civil rights, recruit the feckless to join the mob.

When I look back to the Alabama of my childhood—the hard work on my grandfather's farm, the fast cars speeding home for a visit—it is clear to me that my family, like so many others, knew how to take care of themselves. They were strong, proud, independent men

---

[115]   Bickel, *The Least Dangerous Branch*, 266.

and women. I am not suggesting that inflicting fear and desperation is the best sort of training for citizenship. Terrorism in all its aspects should be out of bounds in a civilized society. But the discipline, resilience, and toughness of that earlier time would not be amiss—either in Black communities or in America generally.

At its best, government at all levels can remove obstacles from the path of such people. Perhaps the meme for the present time is not "that government is best which governs least,"[116] but, instead, that government is best which rewards initiative and resilience most.

---

[116] It is unclear if this quote is attributable to either Thomas Jefferson, Thomas Paine, or Henry David Thoreau, who used it without attribution in *On Civil Disobedience*.

4

BRING BACK THE
ROSENWALD SCHOOLS

BY HAROLD A. BLACK, PH.D.

Children are smart and can be taught. They are stuck in failing schools using a failed method of instruction…It is time to recognize that the education of our children is too important to be left to the government.

The astonishingly poor academic performance of students in public schools continues. This poor performance is met with a lack of effort by school administrators and the education establishment to change how students are "taught." Also astonishing is the total absence of criticisms from black politicians and almost all Civil Rights organizations to push for change. Instead, the impetus for change is from parents who want more for their children—as evidenced by the over one million students on waiting lists for charter and private schools. The growing dissatisfaction on the part of parents is in the tradition of their black ancestors who were emancipated from slavery and showed resiliency when confronted with obstacles in their path.

Although the term "greatest generation" was given to those who grew up during the depression and fought World War II, I would argue that the term best applies to the slaves freed from bondage after the Civil War. That generation had meagre possessions, few skills, and were mostly illiterate. Although emancipated, the vestiges of slavery did not disappear overnight. Many former slaves found themselves working for the same people that previously owned them. Some became sharecroppers and became mired in debt. The institutional memory of slavery would continue for years, affecting choices regarding education, mobility, and the social fabric of the former slaves. Indeed, migration and education were credited with disrupting the institutional legacy of slavery, providing a more complete emancipation for the former slaves and their descendants. As a personal example, my father's mother was a domestic in Americus, GA, and would not let her four daughters do any housework, while her three sons washed, cleaned, and cooked. Born in 1880, she said that she was not training the next generation of maids. All of the daughters graduated from Historically Black Colleges and Universities (HBCUs) and became teachers.

Regardless of their condition, the emancipated blacks were free at last. Faced with daunting obstacles, the former slaves displayed resilience and triumphed against seemingly unsurmountable odds. They built churches, founded social and business societies, created businesses and—more importantly—built schools. Sometimes independently and often with the help of white philanthropists, schools were created—mostly in the states of the old confederacy—to educate black children. Indeed, all the private HBCUs were on southern soil. Despite the often-hostile environment, an educated black professional class grew in the segregated south generating physicians, lawyers, inventors, teachers, and businesspeople.

During segregation, there were two separate silos, one black and one white. Blacks generally were constrained to stay within their silo with segregated schools, churches, businesses and neighborhoods. As we used to say regarding the Civil Rights anthem "We Shall

Overcome," white folks didn't mind us overcoming so long as we did not come over. The irony was that when blacks started "coming over," many found that they were educated on par with and often on levels above those of whites. During the Supreme Court ruling on *Brown v. Board of Education* in 1954 that found the doctrine of "separate but equal" unconstitutional, one of the highest-performing schools in segregated Washington, D.C. was Paul Lawrence Dunbar High School, where over 80 percent of its graduates went to college and where most of its teachers had graduate degrees. Many, if not most, of the first blacks enrolled in the major white universities in the deep south were honors graduates from segregated all-black schools, and then from the previously all-white universities. Those students were the latest in the tradition of emphasizing education started by the generation of freed slaves.

Emerging from slavery into freedom, there were at least two avenues advocated for blacks to achieve equality with whites—whether the whites wanted it or not. One way was that of W.E.B. Dubois, who was born free and who favored political change and activism. The other way was that of Booker T. Washington, who was born into slavery and advocated education and entrepreneurship. Washington thought that if blacks were equal to or superior to whites in education and in business, then they would be integrated into American society. To this end Washington founded the National Negro Business League, was principal of Tuskegee Institute, and founded a program to improve black southern rural education through a public-private partnership. These were the Rosenwald schools, where the philanthropist Julius Rosenwald—then president of Sears Roebuck—matched grants to rural areas to build black schools. By the time this program ended in the 1930s, over 5,300 Rosenwald schools had been built in the south. The program ultimately failed due to the lack of support from white school boards.

Blacks were usually relegated to poorly funded segregated public schools. Black education in the south was not universal, and by 1917 only 58 percent of black children aged six to fourteen attended any school at all. Yet it is amazing what was accomplished with poor funding and facilities. Even rural blacks in poorly funded school districts actively lobbied for improvements in the teaching of their children and their facilities.

Rosenwald was but one of many northern philanthropists supporting black southern education. Many supported colleges and preparatory schools, and religious organizations also founded many HBCUs. Not surprisingly, many of the HBCUs were dedicated to educating black teachers to improve the education of black children.

One wonders what Booker T. Washington, Julius Rosenwald, and others dedicated to improving the status of blacks through education would think of the sad state of education in our public schools today. The abysmal reading scores for American students are a national tragedy. Nationally less than 34 percent of fourth graders read at grade level. The state of Massachusetts has threatened to take over the Boston city schools where only 25 percent of black elementary students read at grade level. In Illinois—mostly within the Chicago school system—there are fifty-three schools where *no student was proficient* at grade level in math, and thirty schools where *no student was proficient in reading!* Such results should lead to a mass firing of school administrators, but that will not happen. In fact, there is only silence from black elected officials and Civil Rights groups, indicating that they have no interest in challenging the status quo. Indeed, many are beholden to the teachers' unions for contributions.

Whereas lack of adequate public funding may have been the demise of the Rosenwald schools, public funding is not the issue in most public-school systems. In Chicago it was over $13,000 per pupil. In Boston it was $27,000 per pupil. Instead of confronting the problem, school curricula are turning to "woke" instruction claiming that language and math are racist and sexist. Some states, such as Oregon, are eliminating standards in math, reading, and writing, instead of attempting to bring children up to proficiency standards.

But children are smart and can be taught. Ask any of these children to recite their favorite rap, and they will not only know all the words, they will quickly learn the words of any new song after only a few listenings. I have long said that if we could get rappers to rap *War and Peace*, our children would know Tolstoy in a week. They are stuck in failing schools using a failed method of instruction.

Professor John Stone of Education Consumers Foundation finds that the deficiencies in reading are culture- and economics-based. He charts economic wellbeing versus third-grade proficiency, showing ethnic makeup. In the chart for New York City, charter schools are among the top performers, regardless of ethnic makeup. His charts for public schools in the state of Tennessee show the same relationship. Stone contends that schools are using woke curricula as an excuse for not adequately teaching basic math and reading skills.

I have previously written:

> Poor children who come from homes of parents (or a single parent) who themselves may be poorly educated are at a disadvantage when they first go to school. The teacher speaks a language that is not spoken in their homes. The children must learn English as a foreign language, while they are trying to learn what is being taught in class. These children start at a disadvantage and using current teaching methods, never catch up. It should come as no surprise that the reading scores of these children are dismal regardless of race.

Professor Stone argues that with a change in the teaching method, the proficiency of poor black (and white) children can match those of children from more affluent educated households. The proven method is called Direct Instruction, and it is opposed by the Education Industrial Complex: the textbook writers, publishers, colleges of education, accreditation boards, and teachers' unions.

Some view the solution to the problem as charter schools. There is no doubt that charter schools have shown that children from similar backgrounds can receive an education superior to that provided in the public schools. Thomas Sowell notes that "official statistics show that students in charter schools in Harlem and other low-income minority communities in New York City pass the statewide mathematics tests at a rate more than six times the rate at which traditional public-school students, housed in the same buildings, pass the same test."

The same can be said for private schools. In particular, Catholic schools have consistently outperformed public schools serving the same populations. Recently, Catholic schools have outperformed even charter schools. While living in Washington, D.C., where the disparity in educational achievement was stark, I suggested turning the public school system over to be run by the Catholics but financed by the city. That suggestion is still relevant. As Sowell notes, "Not all of these kinds of schools are successes. But where there are academic successes in black ghettos, they come disproportionately from schools outside the iron grip of the education establishment and the teachers' unions." It is noteworthy that when a charter school fails, the education establishment cheers. When public schools fail, the education establishment demands more money.

Consistent with the teachings of Booker T. Washington and contrary to those of W.E.B. Dubois, advances in education, not politics, have been the key to black achievement, although politics has sometimes played an ancillary role. Black politicians are, in the main, opposed to charter schools and education outside the strict confines of the Education Industrial Complex. Also opposed are black intellectuals on the left, who—with their Ivy League educations—tell poor blacks that their economic plight is due to systemic racism.

It is time to recognize that the education of our children is too important to be left to the government. Recall that parents are increasingly aware of the failure of our education system as evidenced by the demand for more charter schools. It is also encouraging that more states are instituting and/or expanding school choice. Yet in many instances even charter schools are constrained regarding curricula and teaching methods. Given that many parents cannot get their children into charter schools and cannot afford to send their children to private schools, a more radical suggestion would be to revive the Rosenwald schools—with or without the public funding component.

One approach would be to have states fund the Rosenwald schools—if the states would agree to end the dictating of teaching method and curricula. Another approach would be to institute a privately run school system nationwide to begin to replace public education K-12. These schools could be financed by philanthropists in the tradition of Rosenwald and George Peabody. The schools would provide an alternative to the public schools and concentrate on teaching the basics, using methods like Direct Instruction proven to successfully educate children. Motivation and discipline should be the hallmark of the new Rosenwald schools.

That at-risk children can be successfully taught should attract teachers who are motivated to make a difference in students' lives. Such schools should also motivate parents and guardians to become active in their children's education, through PTAs and at-home learning. Administrators would be held accountable and rewarded if their students achieve success.

Funding would be sought from black billionaires and others interested in education and from those foundations interested in teaching and learning and not in indoctrination. Schools would be evaluated on a regular basis and administrators would be rewarded or replaced based on pupil performance. The best method of instruction would be utilized and would not be dictated to the schools. The state boards of accreditation would be ignored. Too often, those boards are in league with and part of the Education Industrial Complex and are not interested in educating students. Indeed, one school superintendent told me that Direct Instruction would be rejected by the state's accreditation board because it contained *too much reading*.

Graduates of the new schools with solid training in math, English, language, history, civics, and science would likely be motivated to continue their education at the best colleges and universities in the country. In particular, I favor these students going to universities—hopefully HBCUs—that have not succumbed to lowering standards and dumbing down education though I would wager that academic standards even at some HBCUs, like those of most colleges and universities, have been lowered over time. The new Rosenwald foundations would award grants to HBCUs to enhance faculties, facilities, and curricula. If HBCUs strengthen their standards, they would attract the best and most talented students. Then they can take their place as the elite citadels of higher education in an increasingly bleak educational landscape.

This picture is of Dr. Harold Black's grandmother's graduating class in 1906 at Ballard Normal School (later Ballard Hudson High School) in Macon, Georgia. Dr. Black's grandmother is third from the right, front row.

5

CAN I LIVE?

BY RW JONES,
CAN I LIVE, INC.

U.S. entitlement programs are life-stealers and dream deniers. One of our missions is to educate welfare-dependent communities about the loopholes and opportunities in the system that they can use to advance and not have to go homeless or hungry while they advance. We also work with welfare agencies, providing workshops that will help them shift from being agents of dependency to stewards of self-sufficiency.

The welfare system emerged in the 1930s to offset the effects of circumstances like disabilities, old age, a poor education, or unemployment, and to help people get on stable ground. However, as a young, single mother, I realized that the welfare system restrains people that look like me from discovering how to obtain financial independence and reach their dreams. Policies within this system undermine the advancement of not just the current generation, but subsequent ones as well. Angry and disillusioned by this realization, I broke down many times, crying, *"God, are they even human!?"* Knowing that the regulations and the restrictions written by the policy architects did not just affect me, but my children and their dreams, I asked God for a path of escape from this giant. Now, as an entrepreneur, I give people keys so they can be who they were created to be, not who the struggle to live has made them become.

How did I, a woman working in a juvenile correction center, who knew the struggles facing children of single mothers, end up with four sons by three different men? My job was to counsel girls in pregnancy prevention. How did I become one of them?

The struggle had gotten to my mind. I decided to give up, and I had a plan: after I drowned my four sons, I was going to kill myself so I would not have to go to prison. I ran the water and got the towels to wrap their dead bodies in. However, as I was searching the house for my boys so I could implement my plan, I had a literal "but God" moment. In that moment of terror with only split seconds to decide who I should drown first, my children were hidden from my natural sight. After searching, my second son, Nazareth, appeared before me eating a cookie and laughing. Through the laughter, the Lord said, "Wait, hold on, it gets better."

As Nazareth's laughter filled the room and tempered my angry soul, I dropped to the kitchen floor. My almost-crime existed because my foundation had cracked, and I had fallen in. But God came down and sat with me in that crack. After God intervened in my plan to kill my sons and myself, I was able to say, "Let's keep moving, let's keep living and see what unveils." Resilience is God-given, God-breathed.

Years later, I could not bear the thought of being a single mother raising four men all by myself, so I married a man that I knew I had no business being with. I told people, "If I marry this man, know that I am not in my right mind." I married him anyway. *Why did I marry him?* I knew this man was no good, but I had a mindset problem. Later, when I stood back and studied myself, I realized that I was living two different lives—one part of me was propelled to solve a problem, while the other lived on autopilot, preconditioned to a norm that was unbeknownst to my conscious self. I spent hours analyzing, peeling back the layers, talking to God, meditating on where the negative thinking came from, and how and why I had adopted it—when in my heart I disagreed with it. Not wanting to believe I was an anomaly, I looked around and saw that other people operated with this same contradicting mindset—doing what they really did not want to do, becoming someone, a statistic, that they did not want to be.

The way we think allows us to accept what we should reject and be passive when we need to contend or resist. Once we truly see the problems and recognize how we aid and abet the problems, we can do what it takes to break through—to break free and stay free. Once I got my mindset free, I turned my eyes toward the welfare giant that was blocking my dreams.

I saw welfare for what it was: Subtle. Crafty. Cunning. Quietly working against us, while putting on a façade of aid. I realized that the aid does not help us break out of the poverty cycle but keeps us dependent and unfulfilled. "We can't help you pay for law school, but we can support your entrance into a certified nursing assistant program." Being a CNA is fine, but it was not my *dream* and the salary cap for that type of job would keep me poor with four children. That day the door closed to one of my dreams. Unfortunately, the system puts those in need into a compromising position because in order to get some level of assistance, they have to give up a personal goal or dream. To get funding, they have to lower their achievement bar. The trap also denies people real freedom in the form of information that will help them reach their American dream. However, compromising was not an option for me.

The action of resilience looks like never giving up and never taking no for an answer. The mindset of resilience reflects toughness—not being afraid. Even if my sons and I had to live out of a tent or out of my car, I was going to leave the trap and maintain my morality, my integrity, and achieve my destiny. I would not comply, not acquiesce, and not bow to this system that fed itself on dependence.

Can I Live, Inc. is a non-profit organization I founded to help the working poor and the unemployed understand and take advantage of obscure federal opportunities within the HUD Section 3 program. When welfare moms work, they immediately lose access to basic financial assistance—housing vouchers and food stamps. The sad reality is that many of these moms make more money sitting at home doing nothing than they do working. Most of the single mothers we meet do not realize what a bachelor's degree can do and how they can obtain it *while* they are on welfare. In addition, business ownership is a tremendous welfare-slayer, but these agencies do not actively put this type of information into the hands of the nation's poor. HUD has ways to purchase a home with vouchers that they do not advertise. My team and I train people to become active residents in their communities, helping them leverage the resources that exist but are not widely used. We address fatherlessness in the home and show fathers the justice system traps before they step into them.

U.S. entitlement programs are life stealers and dream deniers. One of our missions is to educate welfare-dependent communities about the loopholes and opportunities in the system that they can use to advance—and not have to go homeless or hungry while they advance. We work not only with residents, but also with welfare agencies, providing workshops that will help them shift from being agents of dependency to stewards of self-sufficiency. Understanding the different clientele they serve—from those in situational poverty to those encumbered by generational poverty—is key to resident engagement. Therefore, I provide consulting for housing authorities, service coordinators, and resident services staff who want to increase participation with their programs and see definable outcomes.

As a trailblazer, I have created a map—a blueprint. But people have to *use* the map to set themselves free; I cannot hold their hands in the process. Harriet Tubman gave slaves a time and a place to escape the system of slavery, but they had to leave their plantations and get to the path she was on. Then they had to walk in the direction she pointed, while she went back to find more slaves who wanted to escape. We remind our clients that on their journey resistance will come, and they should not deflect it, run away from it, or deny it, but rather embrace it, because resilience flows in the embracing. Every man and woman can dig deep and find the grit and determination that is going to take them from Point A to Point B.

Within America's poorest communities are men, women, and children who deserve to become who God created them to become. Business owners. Economic visionaries. College degree holders. Affordable housing advocates. Proactive fathers. Policy makers. Resilience stands boldly in the face of a giant system that is wired against our divine purposes and says, "No." Once a person accepts that not every federal or community program has their best interest in mind, they can ask the questions, "How am I going to solve this problem? How am I going to advance, despite my limited educational background and financial resources and despite policies and federal restrictions?"

Our desire is to impact not only welfare moms, the working poor, and stunted dreamers, but to collaborate with current and future business and community leaders on strategies to develop contributors for generations to come. Laws like Section 3 (24 CFR 135) must be simplified for residents who for whatever reason did not complete high school. Our Wealthfair™ Movement rewards action and initiative, which serve as powerful motivators to our young people. By building this movement of residents who refuse to allow others to profit from their pain, not only do we as a people overcome the giant, but we boost confidence, self-esteem and energize dormant dreams.

Our organization is like water in a desert, because the people know we keenly understand their struggle. We lived it. My deputy director once sowed a large financial seed and then lost her job, her apartment, and her car. The employees in the welfare office gave her a tent to go live in a park with her kids. This gesture of "help" was her "AHA!" moment. She realized that the help they give is not the help that is needed. Now she owns a house and has a small business because she used the principles of Can I Live, Inc to climb out of that situation.

With outstretched hands, my team invites everyone to come up and out of their adverse situation. We tell them, "You CAN live!" We carry a conviction that dreams—individual destinies—are worth fighting for. We tell people that the sun might not rise tomorrow, and it might not be next week, but it will come.

I heard God ask me a question when He gave me the name of this organization: "*Can I Live?*" The vexation and earnestness that I heard in His voice made me shudder, because He was expressing how much He wanted to live in the earth and through people. *Can I live in your families? Can I live in your jobs? Can I live in your mindset?* This is His cry, and it is a cry of love. I was shocked when I heard this question, because I thought God could press a button and make anything happen. However, in my spirit, I heard Him explain why He wants to deal justly with these giant systems. "Even *I* am bound by the laws of your land. I live in earthen vessels. If it binds you and denies you, then it denies Me."

These systems are blocking the destinies that He has ordained for us! In addition, when we have bound ourselves—put our loyalties and dependance into these world systems—then we have shut Him out. God knows that if His Kingdom superseded the world's systems, then no one would ever lack. No one would ever be hopeless or homeless. No one would be in bondage. Can I Live, Inc. is an organization that God is positioning to contend specifically with the welfare system. He is inside each of us and where we go He goes because we are His earthen vessels.

I believe that the fulfillment of my purpose is to release God's dream—freedom from captivity—to everyone I meet. Setting the captives free means that many giants have to fall. The welfare system is just one giant. Most if not all of the foundational systems in this country—education, housing, the justice system—have processes that set a cap for each person's advancement and whose traps produce generational poverty. God's justice for these systems means some will fall, and because we have relied so much on these systems, resilience in the aftermath will be our most important virtue.

I will share the freedom message of Can I Live, Inc. to everyone God puts in my path. Partnering with other justice-oriented innovators and giant slayers, I will face the welfare pharaohs and together we will announce, "We don't want your welfare—We Want WEALTHFAIR®!!"[117]

---

[117] Three-year bus tour across America to implement various Can I Live, Inc. programs in poor communities.

6

A POLITICS OF IDEALISM[118]

BY SHELBY STEELE, PH.D.

*Government interventions only shield people
from necessity, hold out the false promise of safe
harbor, and inadvertently give the impression
that a good argument for entitlement (because of
past victimization) can bring the same results as
hard work, an uncompromising commitment to
education, and a spirit of self-help—values that
actually enable people to prosper in freedom.*

I was born into a family conceived in idealism. Our family would never have existed were it not for the idealisms of racial integration and equality. The lives of my parents—an interracial couple that lived on the black side of America's wall of segregation until they reached the brink of their old age—were animated by idealism. I marched with my parents not only for civil rights but also for world peace.

In the 1950s, there was a forty-mile "peace march" every spring from the Great Lakes naval base north of Chicago to a protest rally

---
[118] The following text is excerpted from *Shame* (Basic Books, 2015), by Shelby Steele, Chapter 17, "A Politics of Idealism."

against nuclear weapons at the famous Chicago Water Tower on North Michigan Avenue, near downtown. My mother would offer me up as a marcher every year. Her only lenience, since I was still preteen, was to send me into the march for only the last twenty miles. After twelve or so grueling miles—in a gesture of Gandhian self-flagellation—we always spent the night before reaching downtown in a homeless shelter that invariably reeked of urine, Thunderbird wine, and disinfectant. The idea was to learn compassion—on the way to banning nuclear weapons. I never resisted much. My mother, I knew, was only steeling me for the rigors of idealism.

And the idealism we pursued was premised on the faith that America—and possibly only America—was a great enough nation to realistically pursue things like racial integration and nuclear disarmament. It was an idealism that grew out of a faith in the timeless principles articulated in the Declaration of Independence and the U.S. Constitution (all the betrayals of these principles notwithstanding). My parents, and their like-minded friends, did not assume that the majestic vision of human freedom promised in America's founding documents was a given. Rather, they saw it as an American potential that would have to be fought for and earned. It was the responsibility of good modern Americans to broaden freedom beyond anything Thomas Jefferson or James Madison could have imagined. So they thought of themselves as people in a kind of vanguard of freedom.

The point is that their idealism was based on identification *with*, not against, America. It was an outgrowth of the American creed. They believed that it was precisely social convulsions like the civil rights movement that expanded freedom. My parents married in Chicago in 1944, in violation of existing law in several other states, and against the better judgment of even some of their close friends, who worried for them. But they had internalized their idealism. Their point, as an interracial couple, was that they were not making a point. They were free Americans, and that was the end of it. Researchers investigating interracial marriage would occasionally appear at our front door asking for a "sociological" interview, only to have my mother smile politely as she—a stickler for good manners—discreetly closed the door on them. We were not to be "studied."

This was also the idealism of the Civil Rights Movement as it developed through the 1950s and into the 1960s. One of the movement's most common signs at protests read simply: "I Am a Man." Martin Luther King's "I Have a Dream" speech was a call to focus on "the content of our character" as the true measure of man. The goal of this movement was to have blacks *join* the society on an equal footing with all other Americans. So King was a reformer rather than a revolutionary—and the leader of arguably America's greatest reform movement ever. He sought to petition the government, not overthrow it. And his point was a simple one: that race should never abridge the constitutional rights of any American citizen. Always it was this idea of individual freedom—as expressed in the Constitution—that provided the political and legal framework for his humanistic idealism.

But then came what I have called America's great Fall. As the catalog of American hypocrisies became longer, more vivid, and more indisputable in the 1960s, America fell from its rather blind faith in its own innocence into the knowledge that it was distinctly *not* innocent. The archetypal fall is always a descent from illusion into reality—in this case from a self-flattering, if forced, sense of innocence into the reality that America had shaken hands with the devil.

Does this mean that America was not also a great nation? Certainly not. But it did mean that even its extraordinary greatness—its unmatched capacity for innovation and productivity, its creed of freedom—was not enough to keep it from shaking the devil's hand. Within its greatness, the all-too-familiar fallibilities of human nature—racism, sexism, militarism, greed, and so on—found ways to manifest themselves. Thus, the charge of characterological evil.

And the almost instantaneous reaction to this Fall was the emergence of a left/liberal counterculture that sought to give America a new idealism—not the freedom-based idealism that I had grown up with, but an idealism of governmental activism that would impose The Good on the country. The old idealism of freedom was stained with The Fall itself.

In the mid- and late 1960s, I changed horses, as it were, from an idealism of individual freedom and equality of opportunity (every white man's birthright) to a new idealism in which governmental activism—in the name of some good like "integration" or "environmental protection"— would try to literally manufacture a desired result. Minorities would be shoehorned into equality with racial preferences. Public schools would be school-bused into integration. Endangered species would live in "protected habitats." And all this only seemed reasonable, given America's fallen state.

It was exactly this insight—that America was fallen and therefore vulnerable to guilt about its past—that gave me a sense of entitlement. Suddenly I was not just owed the same level of freedom that whites enjoyed; I was owed the same life that whites enjoyed. And if there was any disparity between my life and theirs—in income or educational achievement or wealth accumulation—then that was proof of ongoing discrimination. "Disparate impact" became the new measure of injustice. The government was called upon to socially engineer us past such disparities—to come up with policies and programs that would take us from a disparity of results to an equality of results.

It was an inevitable sequence: society's brave acknowledgment of past wrongs fueled a sense of entitlement within minorities that could only be assuaged through governmental activism. This was the new idealism that seduced me in the late 1960s.

The logic seemed so clear: now that the overwhelming wrong done to blacks had been acknowledged, the smart thing for us as blacks was to change the very goal of our protest against America, from the achievement of freedom to the establishment of our entitlement. Our identity as a people who had taken charge of their own fate and honorably fought for and won freedom against all odds, against even an often indifferent government, would give way to an identity grounded in aggrievement, on the one hand, and entitlement on the other. This logic—coming out of the perception that whites were at last ashamed of America's racist past—suddenly became the most powerful leverage American minorities had ever known. In fact, white guilt over the past was literally the measure of minority leverage. Freedom was good, but now we had the leverage to demand an actual equality of results. Even as a college student I felt the power of this idea.

But there was a catch. The leverage we gained by relying on America's sense of fallenness came at the price of taking on, and then living with, an identity of grievance and entitlement. I did not understand at the time that this was a fool's bargain, a formula for self-defeat—that it drew minorities into a Faustian pact by which we put our fate in the hands of contrite white people. Very often they were honorable people who simply found it hard to live with history's accusation that they were racist, people who wanted to shout: "Other whites, yes, but not me."

The problem was that, in taking this route, we relinquished considerable control over our own destiny. Rather than seizing as much control over our fate as possible after our civil rights victories of the 1960s, we turned around and looked to the government for the grand schemes that would result in our uplift. It was the first truly profound strategic mistake we made in our long struggle for complete equality. It made us a "contingent people" whose fate depended on what others did for us. Thus it relegated us to the sidelines of our own aspirations. It left us pleading with the government, not for freedom, which we had already won, but for "programs" and "preferences" that would be a ladder to full equality. The chilling result is that now, fifty years later, we remain—by most important measures—in the position of inferiors and dependents.

However, even as I first embraced this new idealism/liberalism, I felt its paternalism to be far more maddening and smothering than anything I had known in full-out segregation. At least after the countless rejections I had endured growing up in segregation, there was no (or very little) psychological enmeshment with my oppressors. They didn't expect me to show gratitude and certainly didn't concern themselves with what I thought or felt about them. Whites found their superiority in disregarding the humanity of blacks altogether. And, paradoxically, the absoluteness of this disregard left blacks to their own resources and to the possibility of a defiant, even profound, dignity. We would find ways to assert the fullness of our humanity no matter society's dismissal of us. With the new post-1960s idealism/liberalism, our humanity was not demeaned; it was simply beside the point. In this liberalism, we were more important as symbols and tokens of white innocence than as human beings.

So, for minorities, the bargain such liberals offered was a terrible trap. It required minorities to see white goodwill as the great transformative force that would lift them into the full equality they could never reach on their own. It enmeshed their longings for equality with white longings for redemption. Through this liberalism, the government took a kind of benevolent dominion over the fate of minorities and the poor, not to genuinely help them (which would require asking from them the hard work and sacrifice that real development requires), but to achieve immunity for the government from the taint of the past.

The tragedy here is that this liberalism asks minorities to believe that the inferiority imposed on them is their best leverage in society—thus making inferiority the wellspring of their entitlement and power even as it undermines the incentive to overcome it. This is the dynamic that causes post-1960s liberalism to mimic precisely the same hierarchical patterns that the ideology of white supremacy imposed—whites as superiors; minorities as inferiors who must be redeemed through the agency of others.

By the mid- to late 1970s I had begun, almost surreptitiously, to hear other voices and to listen to other ideas. I knew very clearly that I still stood for that freedom-focused idealism I had grown up with, the idealism that had animated the original Civil Rights Movement. I still wanted the same things from my society—not special or preferential treatment, not big interventionist programs that would presume to engineer me into equality; just equality under the law, and the unequivocal right to pursue the American dream as I saw fit within the law.

Increasingly—and to my great surprise—I found the idealism I believed in more in what conservatives were saying than in what liberals said. Conservatives didn't want to take you over, make you a pawn in some abstract policy goal, like "integration" or "diversity." They wanted to apply the discipline of freedom to problems of race and poverty and even to the problems of the great middle class. They understood that freedom was equal opportunity in itself. What had to end were the evils of persecution and discrimination, the eternal enemies of freedom. After these enemies were pushed back (and this came to pass), it was up to minorities to fully find their way into the modern world.

No doubt, remnants of the old evils would remain, but they would not be enough to dissuade minorities of their aspirations. I found conservatism, unlike liberalism, to offer the stark fairness of true freedom in which both success and failure are always possible, a fairness of disinterested equanimity. In this kind of fairness there was respect for minorities as people who could be competitive with all others once they were spared persecution and discrimination. Surely it would take some time to make up for the deficits that centuries of oppression had caused, but only the impartiality of true freedom—uncontaminated by group preferences and governmental paternalism—would provide exactly the right incentives to do precisely this.

Government interventions only shield people from necessity, hold out the false promise of safe harbor, and inadvertently give the impression that a good argument for entitlement (because of past victimization) can bring the same results as hard work, an uncompromising commitment to education and a spirit of self-help—values that actually enable people to prosper in freedom. Plain, disinterested freedom clarifies all of this. So yes, conservatism offers minorities a starker freedom than liberalism does—a "flat freedom," like a flat tax that treats everyone exactly the same. But this is a good thing, because it reinforces the values that minorities will most need in freedom. It puts their fate back into their own hands and spares them the illusion of deliverance by others.

7

HOPE IS EVERYTHING

BY ISMAEL HERNANDEZ

When we create the context of liberty and systems that reflect the rational and volitional nature of every person, we discover a universe of possibilities and poverty ceases to be destiny...We also understand that our race is not at the heart of our identity. Every small step opens up a tiny new realm for the possibility of truly autonomous action...We are not drops in a wave. We are an ocean of possibilities.

Aristotle once said that wonder lies at the beginning of philosophy, and it seems to me that similarly, hope lies at the beginning of human flourishing. A people without hope languishes and then perishes. It is in the languishing that we can see the most desperate of all human conditions, as those who struggle cannot see the landscape of possibilities that lies ahead. Their subjectivity—their capacity to be a subject that acts rather than an object that is acted upon—is impaired by fear and by assumptions about their destiny that rob their future. They are deceived to think that hope is a punishment, a dangerous sentiment to be avoided so as to escape disappointment.

The very existence of black people in this country is an icon of hope. Striving against overwhelming odds, they survived the alienating experience of being severed from their kin group and sold to complete strangers who shipped them like cargo. Then came the dreadful middle passage and the beginning of new hardships. The journey stimulated the creation of a new identity in a foreign land. Being in bondage in Africa was followed by ignominious slavery in America, but the enslaved never abandoned their effort to reduce their marginality and re-socialize within a new community. Fugitive slaves braved dangerous escape attempts, but the mass of slaves simply worked, day in and day out, while raising their families under terrible circumstances, not even legally owning their own bodies or the fruits of their labor. They tried to learn and build in hopeful expectation, even when there was no good reason to expect a better life. Still, they hoped and envisioned the day when they not only would enjoy corporate status within America but even experience personal freedom, a privilege denied to both slaves and most non-slaves all over the world. In his autobiography, *Up From Slavery*, Booker T. Washington gives us a glimpse of the hope that fermented in the heart of every slave:

> I had no schooling whatever while I was a slave, though I remember several occasions I went as far as the schoolhouse door with one of my young mistresses to carry her books. The picture of several dozen boys and girls in a schoolroom engaged in study made a deep impression upon me, and I had the feeling that to get into a schoolhouse and study in this way would be about the same as getting into paradise.[119]

---

[119] Booker T. Washington, *Up From Slavery* (Garden City: Dover Publications, 1995).

Having been deemed subhuman chattel, this people still strived and hoped. Their slavery was but the scenery in the drama of their perseverance. Hope came from the strong inner core of their beings as they forged their American identity. That identity owes more to the shared spiritual and moral strength formed through their experience than to the degradations imposed on them. Although outwardly it seemed as if their worth derived from the practical utilitarian exigencies of being possessed by another, in reality it came from within, and that inner worth was indestructible.

The Source of Hope, and Its Abandonment

For a people to have hope, they must know what the good is. The good consists of those intelligible, right, and desirable qualities we perceive in things. The good must be knowable and reachable, and the habit of pursuing it is called virtue. Virtue is a difficult, arduous apprenticeship, because often our lower inclinations fight against the dictates of reason. Yet, it is possible to reach it. Just imagine how desperate human existence would be if we could perceive these necessary qualities only as empty abstractions. Despair would constitute the very essence of our existence as we long for and pursue the unattainable.

The passion of hope is simply the human inclination toward the pursuit of the goods of this world as we journey into eternity. This passion exists because it is connected to certain truths about the human constitution. The classic conception of human nature tied an "ought" to the reality of an "is." There is a law written in the heart of human nature—a law that, as the fifth-century presbyter Lucidus described, is "the first grace of God." In pursuing these goods we can develop habits of action that perfect the nature of human beings. The danger of the skepticism that now informs our body politic is its distrust of the very existence of purpose that is built into the fabric of human nature—because it assumes that there is no human nature. There seem to be only ideas in our minds which threaten to dissolve the good into empty words and rationalizations about power struggles expressed in narrative discourse. This type of discourse provides a structured conception of anecdote; that is, it is a type of fiction. In this view, humans produce meaning by way of anecdote, which is prior in the mind and not in the nature of things. We discover nothing about ourselves, we create everything; we invent meaning and purpose and impose it via power. Now, if there is not a knowable and objective world of values and virtues, how can the contemplation and pursuit of goods such as justice, beauty, and goodness be possible? Can we have authentic hope? If "ought" cannot be derived from "is," what is the basis for human action, right and wrong, legal systems, or virtuous living? In the hands of a skeptical culture, hope dies, while the hordes sing revolutionary songs and praise the death of the old order.

We have thus descended into a neo-Marxist and postmodernist erasure of hope by way of radical claims about what it means to be human. Anthropology remains at the heart of all our controversies. We are told that human goods, if they exist, do not derive from inherent facts about human nature, but are socially construed. We are in a war of one against the other, because war is all there is in the pursuit of power. Human beings do not think or feel, nor is reason "the sovereign architect of the order of knowledge," as Kant put it. Humans are beings only because we assign that meaningless label to the facticity of purposeless matter.

Absent such a thing as nature itself, there is no human nature and no objective goods to pursue, human or otherwise. In the absence of goods, there is no hope. Absent hope, there is no impetus for habits to pursue its objects—that is, there is no virtue. It follows that theories and visions recognizing power as the key element in social, political, cultural, and racial interaction are unable to offer hope to a people whose very social identity was built by hope. They cannot assist us in the creation of a flourishing environment where there is a strong protection for the dignity of human beings. The fate of black Americans and of all human beings lies in the dictates of the powerful, and as such, we remain within the slavery system's paradigm. Maybe today those with power deign to recognize our dignity, maybe tomorrow they rescind it. Modern neo-Marxist theories sprung from more ancient errors can only offer antagonism as the instrument to acquire power in a journey undertaken by beings who are no more than curious accumulations of atoms destined for nothingness. Hope is reduced to an insubstantial word that gives us a good feeling.

The main political, cultural, and intellectual patterns of thought and action in the West today are patterns of deconstruction. Our epistemology is being altered and with it the patterns of thought that seek to classify and explain entities. This transformation thus leads to a change in our ontology. Claims about the nature of being and existence are altered and with them claims about the most important object of inquiry: man himself. We seem to no longer know what reality is, nor what the human person is in the context of existence. Inevitably, our praxis is changing, both legally and culturally. Due to this shattering activity, we can barely recognize ourselves.

Marxism in Black America

Of all challenges to the Western tradition of thought, the most successful in practical terms has been the Marxist. In black America, orthodox Marxism came to dominate minor sectors of the black intellectual class early on, W. E. B. Du Bois and Paul Robeson being prime examples. The excesses of Leninism, and later Stalinism, in Russia made it necessary to explain not only Marx, but the Soviet debacle itself. In the United States, the "New Left" emerged after the death of Stalin in 1953 and constituted a revival of hopes for a metamorphosis of socialism. Marxists fantasized that at last the solution to the conundrum of the mixture of socialist economics with a total-itarian state was at hand. The Promethean project of a new reign of justice was finally possible. The cause of blacks became the most important axis of that aspiration, because it embodied the most severe aspects of capitalist oppression.

Eventually, a challenge to the more reformist approach of Dr. Martin Luther King emerged within the Civil Rights Movement, a development that was informed by the ideas of the New Left. Although not all challenges to King's leadership were Marx-inspired, the Marxist type seems to have eventually dominated this alternative movement. Anti-Americanism and classic Marxist theory contin-ued to inform this transformation of the movement, but elements of neo-Marxist thought were present and moving fast. Race began to be conceived not as an epiphenomenon of class but as a basic reality of identity, irreducible to any other element. Racial identity rather than class consciousness became the focus. "Whiteness" became the prin-cipal scourge of humanity. The key to solving the problem of capital-ist oppression was to "abolish the white race."

Some new theories emerging within Marxism seem to propose a return to a more Hegelian system. This return to Hegelianism does not conclude with the postmodern erasure of identity or its elitist and academic attitude of nihilistic despair at the state of existence, which envisions no political solution. The postmodern critique has been infused with a tool for action—a new praxis, with identity as the weapon. Identity, now collectivized and expanded into multiple axes, serves as the engine for social action under a new designation, "social justice." As power and knowledge determine social reality, activism is the new sacrament conveying the indelible mark of authentic revo-lutionary zeal. The new "liberationist paradigm" is being internalized within the whole culture. Its task of separating identity from biol-ogy remains, but identity is now seen as formed against the backdrop of oppressive social constructs—such as knowledge, language, and power—all of them exploited by the powerful.

The ideas of an era as expressed in its culture are seen now as essential to bringing about the revolution, and these various axes are not reducible to class. Among the movements advocating these new theories we find the Frankfurt School of Critical Theory, Gramscian theories commonly known as "cultural Marxism," and what we can loosely call the "Social Justice" movement. A thousand cuts into the bleeding body of Western civilization will cause its death.

What remains as the key-tying thread in this revolutionary enterprise is the will to power. Gone is any totalizing metanarrative that explains change, such as Marx's metanarrative of class conflict. Gone is the certainty that there is a coherent or even scientific logic to social change. A post-structuralist mood has increasingly taken hold over the whole enterprise of revolution. A will to power is now expressed in a refusal to be governed even by the nature of reality. Everything we once took for granted is to be challenged, because all of it is oppressive. Objective reality, traditional morality, morality itself and even the very understanding of being are social constructs that create a social law imposed by power.

What is more radical and frightening is that there are no rules governing revolutionary phases, as there were in orthodox Marxism. An epistemology of random discontinuity is supreme. All that matters is the devastating hurricane of change and the radical view of the human person's identity described ideologically. Blackness becomes a raw decree from those in power, the idolatry of ideology consuming all and erasing or adding melanin at will. Grand theory necessitates an order in the mind, a rational assessment of processes. Who needs that! What is needed is what Nietzsche identified as key to social existence: the will to power. Critical theory applied to the question of race is an example of the will to power that rejects the need for a coherent metanarrative with logical sequence. Revolution does not need coherence—it needs activism. As Carl Trueman writes, "All previous metanarratives have, for good or ill, attempted to provide the world with stability, a set of categories by which cultures can operate." The new radicalisms reject the need for an epistemology that is seen as part of the very system whose eradication is sought. As Noelle Mering tells us, "The point is to destabilize, fragment, and eradicate hierarchy, history, meaning, and fundamental human identity."

Black feminist thought generated the most radical modes of neo-Marxism now informing our notions of race. Black feminists began to analyze the roles of class, sex, and race as distinct forms of oppression. Early on, feminists had analogized sexism and racism. In 1904, Mary Church Terrell emphasized that in the double jeopardy of sex and race, black women had the lowest hand because they were women: "Not only are colored women…handicapped on account of their sex, but they are almost everywhere baffled and mocked because of their race. Not only because they are women but because they are colored women." Reflecting the longstanding competition for the place of lumpen in the paradigm of oppression, by 1988 black feminist Deborah King observed, "Still others have suggested that heterosexism or homophobia represent another significant oppression and should be included as a third or perhaps fourth jeopardy." Her words witnessed the emergence of additional claims of similar oppressed axis status that now number in the dozens.

So radical is this system of multiple axes of oppression where race is primary in a maze of identities, that only blacks can explain the significance of their oppression. And, as race is an ideological construct, blacks are only those whose consciousness aligns with the progressive political and racial zeitgeist, giving them an epistemically privileged position. Objectivity in the analysis of social reality is merely the academic expression of oppression by a system informed by Whiteness through a "Eurocentric-Masculinist knowledge validation process." This process determines everything with one aim in mind: the maintenance of the balance of power. Liberation only comes by rejecting the mirage of objectivity and acknowledging the epistemic advantage of members of the oppressed group, whose perspective cannot be questioned without unjustly injuring them. The epistemology of scientific research, called positivist by radical feminists, is challenged because it requires distance between the inquirer and the subject of inquiry. Patricia Hill Collins rejects the scientific method because it "asks African American women to objectify themselves, devalue their emotional life, displace their motivations for further knowledge about Black Women, and confront in an adversarial relationship, those who have more social, economic and professional power than they." In other words, what black feminists proposed and later has been extended to the entire spectrum of social science—including questions of class, gender, and race—is adherence to collectivist and unfalsifiable ideological epistemology.

A Return to the Person

Abandoning the totalistic poison of neo-Marxism will help us fight the politics of despair and bring hope to our people. A return to the person—unique and unrepeatable, with the *Imago Dei* imprinted in our being—is the critical step away from the nightmarish idealism of radicalism and all its monsters. I abandoned these monsters long ago, as I journeyed from my island of Puerto Rico to southern Mississippi, of all places. I was a young, black, communist kid who hated America, landing in Dixie! Here, over time, I was confronted with new ideas and a new experience. A new anthropological lens allowed me to realize that I was not merely a drop in the ocean, whose dignity existed strictly within the wave of revolution. I was instead a subject whose dignity was intrinsic—not determined by being a specimen of a group. That experiential encounter with liberty is the antidote to radicalism. Although my new home was an imperfect country by any measure—as all societies are—I discovered that I was a free, volitional, and rational being who is capable of self-determination and irreducible to a mere component.

Our task in black America is to help people discover the grandeur of their personal dignity, one that inheres in them, not one bestowed on them by external agents. When we create a context for our uniqueness to express itself, an amazing and undirected process of improvement begins.

Liberty as the sum of all our freedoms can come only from newly reaffirming an old anthropology that recognizes our capacity to scrape into the dirt of the ground and, through the sweat of our brow and the insights of our minds, create value for ourselves and for others. When we create the context of liberty and systems that reflect the rational and volitional nature of every person, we discover a universe of possibilities, and poverty ceases to be destiny. The poor are no longer merely mouths to be fed, bodies to be clothed, and problems to be solved. We also understand that our race is not at the heart of our identity. Every small step opens up a tiny new realm for the possibility of truly autonomous action. We must believe this, proclaim it boldly, and teach it widely. Even more importantly, we must help people experience this reality through simple and practical projects that position them, as individuals, as protagonists of their development, instead of remaining passive, like scenery in the drama of historical forces outside their control or tokens of pity or magnanimity. We are not drops in a wave. We are an ocean of possibilities.

EPILOGUE
RECOVERING HOPE
BY JOSHUA MITCHELL, PH.D.

You have finished reading a book that is occasionally rough but always hopeful. The prose is straight-forward and at times blunt. It tells of unvarnished struggles that end in triumph—some small and some grand—of those who have succeeded against almost unimaginable odds. It also presents the insights and wisdom of scholars who have studied and can explain the forces that once produced success, as well as those that now threaten it. The book speaks to the richness, complexity, agony, and joy of life, which no statistical tables can convey.

What shines through on every page is resilience and hope. Collectively, the essays offer a blueprint for how all Americans can work together to build a peaceful and prosperous future—for all its people.

There are three important themes in *Red, White, and Black: Vol. 2*. Compelling testimony and direct evidence are presented by the grassroots leaders of the Woodson Center's network who overcame unimaginable barriers—some circumstantial, some of their own making. Added to this is the wisdom of scholars: noted black educators, a retired prominent jurist, civic leaders, and successful entrepreneurs. Some provide important insights into the often ignored but amazing achievements of blacks in America from slavery on—in education, commerce, and civil rights. And others point to the dangerous forces that threaten to destroy these positive movements and shackle the ability of blacks to succeed today.

What is resilience, and why write about it today? More precisely, why write a second book, after the notable success of The Woodson Center's previous book, *Red, White, and Black*?[120] What more needed to be said? Although the first book has an internal coherence of its own, it was written to respond, as many others did, to *The 1619 Project* of Hannah Nicole Jones,[121] published by the *New York Times*. Why her long-form article took hold of the American imagination as powerfully as it did will be debated for years to come. Its central claim—that since the first slaves were brought ashore in Jamestown in 1619, America has been *systemically* racist—was defended by many and attacked by a few. Was it the case, as she claimed, that slavery, Jim Crow, and the current plight of a notable portion of black America have a single cause?

Red, White, and Black did not claim that America was pure and not irredeemably stained. Rather, it argued that the story told by *The 1619 Project* overlooked, perhaps deliberately, black success in America, in spite of the obvious obstacles that had existed. *Red, White, and Black* also contended that the mid-twentieth century trajectory that suggested an approaching parity between blacks and whites in America was disrupted by The Great Society programs of the 1960s, which undermined the mediating institutions of family and church which *every* group of Americans needs, not least those communities under stress. Systemic racism was not the real cause—government attempts to "help" had disrupted the social fabric of black American communities by undermining the very institutions that had held black America together at a time when the State *really was* against them. This new

---

[120] Robert L. Woodson, *Red, White, and Black: Rescuing American History from Revisionists and Race Hustlers* (Brentwood: Emancipation Books, 2021).
[121] Jones, "The 1619 Project."

volume presents thoughtful commentary by new voices, who outline, firsthand, the damage done by those who embrace the notion that black adversity continues to be the product of systemic racism and is, as a consequence, unchangeable and therefore no one, including blacks, need step up to the realities of a responsible life. Our scholars outline how that dangerous thinking is beginning to permeate our government social systems and even our judicial system.

Time passed after the successful publication of *Red, White, and Black, Vol. 1*. The monthly Zoom meetings over which Bob Woodson presided, which brought together academics and practitioners from across the country and which had produced a compelling answer to *The 1619 Project*, continued, but the tone changed. What emerged was a sense of urgency, no longer about answering it directly, but about the sense of *hopelessness* that underlies the claim that there are systemic forces, of any source, aligned against American citizens, which force them into impotence and despair.

We can argue about the history of slavery in America and its aftermath, but the moral question that still rests on us, regardless of the position we take, is this: Are resilience and hope possible in the midst of adversity, however grave? If the adversity is systemic, then the answer is likely not only to be "no," but also that *the State alone* has the resources to overcome it. This frame of mind seems very much to have captivated the American imagination recently, and not only about race. Systemic forces of globalism are said to be aligned against the middle class. Climate change is said to make individual action impossible; only systemic global coordination can "save the planet." Americans have increasingly become hopeless, not just about race, but about their future—about everything. Individuals, friends, families, local civics groups, churches, local governments—are these now irrelevant to human thriving? The answer that Bob Woodson's Zoom participants gave was a resounding "NO!"

The practitioners—many of whom have written chapters in this book—gave the most emphatic answer. They do not do this by making arguments, but by providing evidence. Hard evidence: Like the mother who turned the tragedy of her beloved daughter's senseless death into a mission to help other bereaved mothers become agents of peace and positivity in their communities. Like those who used their own troubled life experiences to help others escape lives of drugs, crime, and violence. There are amazing stories of courage and determination: the homeless girl who put herself through school and is now an airline pilot, and the virtually unknown three black barbers of history who helped thousands of slaves escape to Canada.

The scholars provide further evidence and valuable insights: how the Rosenwald schools created extraordinarily high levels of academic achievement; how black business enterprises thrived in hostile times; and how black associations pooled their resources to provide insurance funds, investment capital, and sources of loans. A retired judge recounts the painful history and the gritty perseverance of blacks in the fight for Voting Rights in Alabama; others recount unique examples and lessons in success in television, or in personal lives.

There is a call to action in these essays—action to ensure our national polities do not ignore this rich history of resilience and achievement and further to ensure that current policies based on misguided assumptions will not be permitted to stifle the initiatives that are fundamental to the success of all Americans.

Today, Americans of every stripe hunger for evidence that resilience matters, that hope matters, that adversity is *not* the final word, that they are not the playthings of systemic forces they can neither control nor fully understand. Those who have written chapters in the book break our fast and provide the first food to sate our hunger. It is enlightening, inspiring, and most importantly, provides a pathway to the future.

A final word about what should lie ahead, for all Americans. Seek out resilience. To find it, look in the places where you live. More precisely, look in the places you think it cannot be found. Resilience surprises. Then, quietly and behind the scenes, support it—with your time and with your funds. Bob Woodson reminds us that "the solutions to the problems communities face reside in those communities." Evidence of resilience is not far away; it is right next door, where you least expect it. This book, too, has something unexpected about it. More than chapters to be passively read, *Resilience* is an invitation and a promissory note—it points directly to what American renewal might *really* involve. No political party or government program can initiate it. The miracle of American democracy, Alexis de Tocqueville wrote almost two centuries ago, is that it is capable of "unleashing an energy never before seen in human civilization." He understood, as the authors of the chapters in this book do, that the energy of this nation can only be released through the face-to-face relations we encounter and fortify within our immediate community. Let us make good on that prophecy. It is not late in the day. It is early. We have work to do. We have hope to recover.

ACKNOWLEDGMENTS

Many people contributed to the publication of this book and the continued success of the Woodson Center, including of course our scholars and grassroots practitioners whose essays are presented here. I would make special mention of our brother Bishop Dean Nelson, who recently passed but remains with us in spirit. In addition, I would like to acknowledge the people whose decades of labor behind the scenes have made all of this possible. My executive assistant, Hattie Porterfield, our longtime CFO Stephanie Detrio, our bookkeeper Phyllis Stukes, retired COO Terence Mathis, retired CAN director Curtis Watkins, events coordinator Maria Brazda, and special training consultant Charles Perry. These dedicated people are now passing the baton to the next generation of staffers to carry on the important work of serving the least of God's children.

Special thanks also to Beth Feeley, who helped the Center launch the 1776 Unites project, our quarterback COO Julia Nelson, and Heather Humphries who assisted with editing this volume and has been a valuable ally since the Center's beginning.

ABOUT THE AUTHORS

Editor

Robert L. Woodson, Sr. is founder and president of the Woodson Center and an influential leader on issues of poverty alleviation and empowering disadvantaged communities to become agents of their own uplift. He is a frequent advisor to local, state, and federal government officials as well as business and philanthropic organizations.

His social activism dates back to the 1960s, when, as a young civil rights activist, he developed and coordinated national and local community revitalization programs. During the 1970s, he directed the National Urban League's Administration of Justice Division. Later he served as a resident fellow at the American Enterprise Institute.

Woodson is frequently featured as a social commentator in print and on-air media, including C-SPAN, CNN, *Tucker Carlson Tonight*, *Meet the Press*, *The O'Reilly Factor*, and other national and local broadcasts. He is a contributing editor to the *Hill* and the *Wall Street Journal* and has been published in influential newspapers and journals, such as *Forbes*, *National Review*, the *Washington Post*, *Milwaukee Journal Sentinel*, *Harvard Journal of Law & Public Policy*, *Vanderbilt Law Review*, and other national and local media outlets.

He is the recipient of the prestigious John D. and Catherine T. MacArthur "Genius" Fellowship Award, the Bradley Prizes presented by the Lynde and Harry Bradley Foundation, the Presidential Citizens Medal, the 2018 William Wilberforce Award, and many other awards and honors.

Woodson is the author of several books, including *On the Road to Economic Freedom: An Agenda for Black Progress* and *The Triumphs of Joseph: How Today's Community Healers are Reviving Our Streets and Neighborhoods.*

Contributors

Joshua Mitchell, professor of government at Georgetown University, Senior Fellow at the Woodson Center, and Senior Fellow at the Common Sense Society has written extensively about the need to refortify America's mediating institutions. From 2005 to 2020, he was actively involved with Georgetown's School of Foreign Service in Doha, Qatar; and from 2008-10 he took leave from Georgetown and was the Acting Chancellor of The American University of Iraq-Sulaimani.

Ismael Hernandez is the founder and president of The Freedom & Virtue Institute, whose mission challenges the paternalistic, condescending, and statist processes that attempt to address poverty in America. His writings have appeared in various newspapers as well as *Crisis Magazine*, *World Magazine*, the *Washington Times*, the *Vital Center*, and the *Schweizer Monat Magazine* in Switzerland. Hernandez is a member of the Board of Scholars of the 1776 Project and lectures for the Acton Institute in Grand Rapids, Michigan. He wrote *Not Tragically Colored: Freedom, Personhood, and the Renewal of Black America*, and he recently co-authored *Race and Justice in America*. Ismael holds a master's degree in political sciences and lives in North Carolina with his family.

Glenn C. Loury is Merton P. Stoltz Professor of Economics at Brown University. As an economic theorist, he has published widely and lectured throughout the world on his research. Loury is among America's leading critics writing on racial inequality. He has been elected as a Distinguished Fellow of the American Economic Association, as a Member of the American Philosophical Society and of the U.S. Council on Foreign Relations, and as a Fellow of the Econometric Society and of the American Academy of Arts and Sciences.

Dr. Phillip D. Fletcher is the founder and chief executive officer of The City of Hope Outreach (CoHO) in Conway, Arkansas, an organization that provokes hope in individuals, families, and communities for the glory of God. He serves as adjunct professor of ethics at Philander Smith University, an HBCU. Dr. Fletcher addresses issues of leadership, ethics, and social issues through the philosophy of personalism. He authored *The Excellence of God: Essays on Theology and Doxology* published by Crossbooks, and self-published *Created in Freedom: Poverty and Economics* and *Angst and Hope: Protest, Pandemic, and Politics*. In 2015, Governor Asa Hutchinson appointed Dr. Fletcher to the 20th Judicial District Criminal Detention Facilities Review Committee. In addition, he hosted the AETN-PBS television program; *A Deeper Look: The Poverty Divide* in Arkansas and was recognized as one of Arkansas' Top Professionals in 2021 by *Arkansas Money and Politics*. A native of Louisville, Kentucky, Dr. Fletcher received his BA in Ethnic Studies from the University of California at Riverside, MA in Theology and Apologetics from Liberty University, and doctorate in Organizational Leadership from Regent University.

Racquel Williams-Jones (RW Jones) is the founder of Can I Live, Inc., and thought leader behind the One Million Moms OFF Welfare Initiative–a strategy which aims to reduce dependency on government subsidies for assisted families. RW advocates for single mothers navigating social services benefits, and leads national conferences, keynotes, and trainings as an expert on community engagement, leadership development, and economic self-sufficiency strategies. RW has led and organized tent cities, volunteered on civic boards, chaired a housing authority, and influenced policy through various commission appointments. An author, motivational speaker, play/short film writer and business thought leader, she holds an MA in Public Administration, a BA in Economics, Politics and Law, and an AA in Criminal Justice emphasizing Juvenile Delinquency.

Harold A. Black is Emeritus Professor of Finance at the University of Tennessee. He was appointed by President Carter to serve on the first National Credit Union Administration Board. Black has published extensively in the leading journals in business and economics. He served on the boards of two of the nation's largest financial institutions and his consulting clients are among the leading law firms and financial institutions in the country. His academic contributions were honored in the Dr. Harold A. Black Academic Conference sponsored by the University of Tennessee, the University of Tennessee at Chattanooga, and Middle Tennessee State University. The University of Georgia's Terry College of Business endowed a named professorship in his honor and named its new freshman dormitory for him and two others who integrated its freshman class in 1966. After, receiving his undergraduate degree from the University of Georgia, he received his PhD from The Ohio State University. His faculty appointments include the University of Florida, Howard University, and the University of North Carolina at Chapel Hill.

Reverend Dean Nelson was a minister and founder of the Douglass Leadership Institute, which educates, equips, and empowers faith leaders to embrace and apply Biblical principles to life and in the marketplace. He also served as Vice President of Government Relations for Human Coalition, a national non-profit serving women and families in metropolitan areas. In 2018, as an appointee of Maryland Governor Larry Hogan, Rev. Nelson served on the Congressional

Frederick Douglass Bicentennial Commission whose mission was to honor the life and legacy of Frederick Douglass. In 2023, he served on the Board of Visitors for the University of Mary Washington as an appointee of Virginia Governor Glenn Youngkin. Rev. Nelson worked with a diverse array of groups including the United Way, NAACP, Prison Fellowship, the SCLC, and TeenPact Leadership Schools. He appeared on and was published in various media outlets, including *World Magazine*, MSNBC, Fox News, ABC, USA Today, CBN and EWTN. A graduate of the University of Virginia, he was a devoted husband and father, and a faithful man of God. Rev. Nelson passed away in December of 2023 after a brief battle with cancer.

Sheena Michele Mason, assistant professor of English at SUNY Oneonta, specializes in Africana and American literature and philosophy of race. Mason is published with Oxford University Press, Palgrave MacMillan, Cambridge University Press, and the University of Warsaw among other presses. She is the innovator of the theory of racelessness, from which she founded an educational firm named Theory of Racelessness. Her book *The Raceless Antiracist: Why Ending Race Is the Future of Antiracism* shows how ending our belief in "race" and practice of racialization is required toward the goal of ending the causes and effects of racialized dehumanization. She holds a PhD with distinction in English literature from Howard University in Washington, DC.

Cynthia Millen (C. M. Millen) has written children's books and poetry for over thirty years, published worldwide through Houghton-Mifflin, Candlewick, Walker Books, Penguin Random House, and Charlesbridge, as well as in numerous literary magazines. She received a Parents' Choice Award for her first book, *A Symphony for the Sheep*, and the Lee Hopkins National Poetry Award for "The Ink Garden of Brother Theophane." Her most recent publications are *Cat in the*

Cathedral (Paulist Press) and a middle school chapter book, *Hinges* (University of Toledo Press), about the Underground Railroad in Northwest Ohio. She and her husband are the parents of five children and seven grandchildren.

Ron Anderson is the Executive Director of Project Reclaim of Louisiana, Inc., which facilitates a juvenile delinquency prevention-based Youth Leadership Academy program for youth, parent training and parental involvement activities for parents and guardians, as well as Optimal Potential Life Skills classes for youth and adults in the court system. Anderson has received numerous awards in the field of public service, including The Volunteers of America "National Leadership" Award, The National Conference of Community and Justice "Brotherhood/Sisterhood Humanitarian" Award, The "Citizen of the Year" Award from the Shreveport Chapter of the National Association of Social Workers, The "Man of the Year" Award from Omega Psi Phi Fraternity, Incorporated, Gamma Omicron Chapter, The "Partner in Education" Award from the Shreveport/Bossier Chapter of Phi Delta Kappa and many other awards and honors. In 2000, he was named "One of the 10 Most Outstanding Leaders of the Community" by the *Shreveport Times*.

Rachel Ferguson is the Director of the Free Enterprise Center at Concordia University Chicago, Assistant Dean of the College of Business, and Professor of Business Ethics. She is an affiliate scholar of the Acton Institute and the Faith and Liberty Discovery Center, and co-author of *Black Liberation Through the Marketplace: Hope, Heartbreak, and the Promise of America.* Her commentary has been featured at *National Review, The Dispatch, Christian Post*, the *Acton Power Blog, Religion & Liberty, Discourse Magazine, Law & Liberty, Profectus,* and others. Ferguson serves on the board of LOVEtheLOU, a neighborhood stabilization ministry in St. Louis, Missouri, as well as the

Freedom Center of Missouri, which advocates for economic freedom cases. She serves in an advisory board role at the apologetics ministry, ReThink315. Ferguson also helped found Gateway2Flourishing, a group of Christian businesspeople dedicated to dignifying forms of philanthropy in the St. Louis area. Rachel lives with her husband, Mike Ferguson, who hosts the morning show on NewsTalkSTL as well as a nationally syndicated interview show, *American Viewpoints*. They have two sons, Asher and Solomon.

John Sibley Butler, the J. Marion West Chair in Constructive Capitalism at The University of Texas at Austin (Emeritus, 2022), researches the development of high-tech centers around the world, innovation, entrepreneurship and organizational science. His extensive work includes *Global Issues in Technology Transfer* (with David Gibson), *Entrepreneurship and Self-Help Among Black Americans: A Reconstruction of Race and Economics, All That You Can Be* (with Charles C. Moskos) and *An American Story: Mexican American Entrepreneurship & Wealth Creation* (with Alfonso Morals and David Torrs). He serves as a consultant for the development of smart cities around the globe.

Michael David Cobb Bowen is known for his work as a writer and commentator, particularly on issues related to politics, culture, and African American interests. He has contributed to the public discourse through various platforms, including blogs, columns, and public speaking. Bowen is also recognized for his involvement in discussions on conservatism within the African American community, providing a perspective that contributes to the broader dialogue on political and social issues in the United States. Bowen is a Stoic, an entrepreneur and author of the award-winning blog *Cobb*. He has been published in *Newsweek* and was a regular NPR contributor, host at *Cafe Utne*, founding member of The Conservative Brotherhood,

Rights Universal, and Free Black Thought. His online writing projects on political, cultural and philosophical subjects go back to the early 1990s making him a pioneer in black-oriented online spaces. His current writing projects can be found at Sub stack: @mdcbowen. Bowen is a staunch civil libertarian, 2A defender, and proponent against all racial theories.

Ian V. Rowe is a Senior Fellow at the American Enterprise Institute; the founder & CEO of Vertex Partnership Academies, a virtues-based, International Baccalaureate public charter high school in the Bronx; and a Senior Visiting Fellow at the Woodson Center. In addition to serving ten years as CEO of Public Prep, he held leadership positions at Teach for America, the Bill & Melinda Gates Foundation, the White House, and MTV, where he earned two Public Service Emmys. With his book *Agency*, Mr. Rowe introduces an empowering framework, F.R.E.E.—Family; Religion; Education; and Entrepreneurship, to inspire young people of all races to build strong families, overcome the victimhood narrative and become masters of their own destiny. Mr. Rowe is Chairman of the Board of Spence-Chapin. He earned an MBA from Harvard Business School, a BS from Cornell University's College of Engineering and his high school diploma from Brooklyn Tech as part of a K-12 NYC public education. Mr. Rowe is a recipient of many honors, including the Harvard Business School Bert King Service Award, and most recently the George A. Sutherland Award.

Jason D. Hill, professor of philosophy at DePaul University in Chicago, specializes in ethics, social and political philosophy, and philosophical psychology. The author of six books including the bestselling, *We Have Overcome: An Immigrant's Letter to the American People* and *What Do White Americans Owe Black People?: Racial Justice in the Age of Post-Oppression*, Hill has been published in major magazines including *The Federalist*, *The American Mind*, *The American Thinker*, *Commentary Magazine*, *Spiked Magazine*, *American Greatness* and *Salon*. He has been interviewed regularly in various media outlets, including NBC's *Today show*, *The Daily Caller Show*, Fox News, Fox Business, Bill O'Reilly's *No Spin News*, NPR, and several other mainstream media. Jason Hill is deeply committed to Moral Foundationalism, Moral Universalism, and the Absolutism of Reason. At the age of twenty, he migrated to the United States from Jamaica and has thrived beyond his wildest dreams. He remains incredibly grateful to this country for its bountiful opportunities.

Sylvia Bennett-Stone serves as a dedicated Servant-Leader and current Director of the Woodson Center Voices of Black Mothers United (VBMU). VBMU is a national movement that brings together mothers of victims of community violence as a force for change. VBMU is committed to addressing deficiencies resulting in community violence and the family's deterioration. When human beings experience trauma or severe life stressors, it is not uncommon for their lives to begin to unravel. Tragically, in 2004 Krystal Joy, her daughter, was the victim of a senseless violent crime. Sylvia discovered great passion in turning her anger and grief into healing power for helping to serve others that experienced a similar tragedy. She began her life-long commitment to uplift lives through her own pain. Sylvia chronicles her own healing journey in her book *Mindfields: A Healing Journey to Survive the Murder of a Child*. Sylvia's approach addresses the healing process first. Next, she helps the mothers develop and implement solutions that address senseless community violence by focusing on her method: "One Block at a Time." She is a national speaker and has been featured in *USA Today*, the *Wall Street Journal*, *Christian Post*, *Essence Magazine*, and numerous national media outlets.

<u>Gary Wyatt</u> is the founder and president of He Brought Us Out Ministry Inc, a non-profit, faith-based community organization which serves the Akron community as the North Hill Community House. Wyatt's book, *From Dealing to Healing*, recounts his inner-city upbringing surrounded by alcohol and drugs and his subsequent addiction to the drugs he sold. Once he came to faith in Christ, his life changed. Wyatt has been featured in the articles, "Ministry Empowers North Hill Community" (*Akron Beacon Journal*, March 2005), and "War on Poverty" (*Wall Street Journal*, April 2005), among others. Since 2001, he and his wife, Patricia, have established tutoring, summer camp, and youth mentoring programs and formed block watches that close neighborhood drug houses. Among his awards and memberships are the YMCA adult Volunteer of the Year (East Akron), the 2009 Charles Salem Humanitarian Award, and the Certificate of Special Congressional Recognition The Honorable Betty Sutton. He was an Advisory Committee board member for the John S. and James L. Knight Foundation, the featured Speaker at the Pepperdine School of Public Policy's "The Quest for Community," and a panelist at The Gerald R. Ford Presidential Foundation Conference, "Strengthening Mediating Structures in Community."

<u>Jon D. Ponder</u>, founder and CEO of HOPE for Prisoners, Inc., established the Nevada-based nonprofit in 2010 to provide the formerly incarcerated with long-term support and services as they work to reintegrate into society. Jon oversees all aspects of the initiatives offered and is responsible for developing and implementing strategic planning for the organization. Because of his leadership, HFP graduates more than 450 clients in Southern Nevada every year, setting them on a path to lifelong success. Formerly incarcerated himself, he is passionate about the value of mentoring for people coming out of correctional settings and he is uniquely equipped to provide guidance and motivation to those navigating the challenges of reentry. Ponder's

leadership has been recognized both statewide and nationally. In 2020, he received both a full Presidential Pardon and a State Pardon from Nevada. Ponder serves on the Nevada Corrections and Law Enforcement Committee and is co-founder of the first-of-its-kind statewide Corrections and Reentry Advisory Council. He also serves as a Commissioner with the Nevada Commission on Postsecondary Education and Nevada Sentencing Commission and as an ordained chaplain with Chaplaincy Nevada.

Yaya J. Fanusie is an expert on U.S. national security issues relating to financial technology. He spent seven years as a CIA analyst where he covered terrorism and economic security threats. During his CIA career, Yaya personally briefed President George W. Bush on terrorism issues and spent time in Afghanistan providing analytic support to senior U.S. military officials. Since government service, Yaya has worked in anti-money laundering consulting, the digital asset industry, and the Washington D.C. national security think tank community. He has testified before Congress multiple times on national security and illicit finance. Before working in government, Yaya taught mathematics at a charter high school in DC. He also served as a budget analyst for DC's school system and juvenile detention administration. In 2018, he taught a course on blockchain technology at Morgan State University, a historically black institution in Baltimore. Yaya is also a creative writer. He produces *The Jabbari Lincoln Files*, a spy thriller podcast drama where the protagonist happens to be an African American Muslim CIA officer. Yaya received an MA in International Affairs from Columbia University's School of International and Public Affairs and a BA in Economics from UC Berkeley.

Charles Love is the Executive Director of Seeking Educational Excellence (SEE), a non-profit dedicated to empowering disadvantaged students to reach their full potential. He is a scholar at 1776 Unites, co-host of the *Cut the Bull Podcast* and the author of several books, including *Race Crazy: BLM, 1619, and the Progressive Racism Movement*. Charles frequently writes on race and cultural issues and is a member of New York City's Community Education Council.

Janice Rogers Brown was confirmed to the U.S. Court of Appeals for the DC Circuit in 2005 and retired from that court in 2017. Her previous positions were Associate Justice of the California Supreme Court, Associate Justice of the Third District Court of Appeals in Sacramento and, the Legal Affairs Secretary to Governor Pete Wilson. Brown serves on the boards of the Coolidge Foundation, the Association of College Trustees and Alumni (ACTA), the Woodson Center and its affiliated 1776 Unites Project, and the Ulysses S. Grant Institute for the Study of Democracy. She chairs the Advisory Board of The New Civil Liberties Alliance and is (occasionally) a visiting professor at the University of California, Berkeley School of Law. Brown has received numerous awards including the Jurisprudence Award of the Claremont Institute's Center for Constitutional Jurisprudence, the Originalism and Religious Liberty Award of the Alliance Defending Freedom, and the Bradley Award. Brown graduated from the University of California, Los Angeles, School of Law and California State University, Sacramento. In 2004 she received a Master of Laws degree in Judicial Process after completing the Graduate Program for Judges at the University of Virginia School of Law.

Kamia Bradley, a twenty-five-year-old airline pilot from Denver, Colorado graduated from Embry-Riddle Aeronautical University in Prescott, Arizona in 2020. She flies the Embraer E-175 aircraft. As a junior in high school, she was honored to be one of the students chosen to ride over Denver in a helicopter, and a passion for flying was sparked. Life's contrasts were magnified when the pilot flew over her home, an apartment with no working heat during Colorado winters and where she slept on the floor. Despite the astounding juxtaposition of the moment, she framed a perspective where her apartment complex became a key part of the masterpiece of the cityscape. "At that moment, I decided that if I could see the whole world from the sky, just like I had seen my apartment complex, I could do anything."

Will Crossley serves as President and CEO of The Piney Woods School, the nation's oldest, continuously operating Black boarding program, which serves deserving youth from across the globe regardless of their ability to pay their way. At the age of twelve years old, Will—a native of Chicago, IL—received a scholarship to attend Piney Woods, and is the first alumnus to serve in this capacity. Prior to his current role, Will received a presidential appointment in the U.S. Department of Education, Office for Civil Rights. Trained as a civil rights attorney, Will has served as Chief Counsel and Director of Voter Protection to the Democratic National Committee, practiced with the law firm WilmerHale, LLP, clerked with federal trial and appellate level courts, and completed a Barton Fellowship in research and teaching at Emory Law School. Prior to his legal career, Will was a policy analyst in the Georgia Governor's Office, an education researcher, and an elementary school teacher. He holds a BA from the University of Chicago, MEd from Harvard University, and JD from the University of Virginia. He resides in Piney Woods, MS, with his wife, Monica, and their two girls, Kayla and Christin.

Brian S. Wade is founder and co-founder of drug and alcohol recovery houses and treatment centers; The Genesis Center, The Alpha House, and The Georgia House. These serve communities in Ohio with holistic, faith-based programs that include SRLP (Sober Residential Living Program), empowering therapy services, and vocational programs. His role has shifted from direct contact with treatment residents to creating and sustaining an organization that supports the team. Wade has a wide-ranging vocational background which includes managing restaurants, working in construction, landscaping, auto mechanics, management, sales, and financial advising. He started and built multiple nonprofits, consulted nonprofit organizations across the U.S., and started and operated multiple businesses. Son of pastors and church planters, he has served in various ministerial capacities and is a consultant to pastors and ministry leaders. Wade is a grateful father and grandfather and devoted husband to Holly, his wife of forty years.

Shelby Steele analyzes race relations, multiculturalism, and affirmative action. The Robert J. and Marion E. Oster Senior Fellow (adjunct) at the Hoover Institution, he has written widely on race in American society and the consequences of contemporary social programs on race relations. In 1991, his work on the documentary *Seven Days in Bensonhurst* was recognized with an Emmy Award. He also received the Writer's Guild Award and the San Francisco Film Festival Award. Steele's books include: *The Content of Our Character: A New Vision of Race in America, Shame: How America's Past Sins Have Polarized Our Country, A Bound Man: Why We Are Excited About Obama and Why He Can't Win, White Guilt: How Blacks and Whites Together Destroyed the Promise of the Civil Rights Era* and *A Dream Deferred: The Second Betrayal of Black Freedom in America.* Steele has written for the *New York Times* and the *Wall Street Journal.* A popular speaker, he has appeared on national current affairs news programs including *Nightline* and *60 Minutes.* Steele holds a PhD in English from the University of Utah, an MA in sociology from Southern Illinois University, and a BA in political science from Coe College in Iowa.